PERSPECTIVE

A STUDY IN THE BOOK OF PHILIPPIANS

STEVE ROBINSON

Perspective Shift: A Study in the Book of Philippians

Copyright © 2023 by Steve Robinson. All rights reserved.

...Let this mind be in you which was also in Christ Jesus.

Philippians 2:5

CONTENTS

WELCOME TO PERSPECTIVE SHIFT

Do you ever feel like you just can't catch a break in life? Your bills are stacking up. Your health's not good. Your relationships are beyond frustrating. You feel tied to negative circumstances and asking yourself, "How did I get here?" "Why did this happen?" "How do I get out of this?" I've been there.

Well, friend, I have good news for you today—you don't have to live broken down and defeated. God created you to experience life and freedom—even when life's circumstances are less than favorable. God gives you the ability to rise above your challenges and to live with supernatural joy. Unfortunately, if you're not intentional, you can live like countless others today – having blurred vision, feeling limited, controlled by your circumstances, and just flat exhausted.

So, how do you change that? Before your circumstances change, you have to change your perspective. We all need a *Perspective Shift*! And, how do you shift your perspective? Well, the New Testament book of Philippians – written by the Apostle Paul – holds the keys. In this study, *Perspective Shift*, we're setting out on a journey to know Christ deeper and to gain practical tools for living life from God's perspective. Let's journey together!

Pastor Steve

Steve Robinson

GETTING THE MOST OUT OF THIS STUDY

This guide is designed with two groups of people in mind. First, for those of you engaged in a spiritual growth campaign with your church. These practical campaigns consist of three elements:

1. **Weekly Sermons**
2. **Weekly Small Group Sessions**
3. **Daily Devotions with Reflection Questions**

Over the past twenty years, we have discovered supernatural growth happens when we combine practical sermons, life-giving small groups, and encouraging daily devotions. We grow in the rows while hearing the Word of God in weekly sermons. We grow in circles as we engage truth and discuss it with like-minded individuals in a small group setting. We grow individually through daily devotions and diving into God's Word. When we combine the three, it leads to exponential growth. However, this growth is not limited to those involved in a spiritual growth campaign.

Second, this can be completed for personal enrichment and growth. However, why not reach out to friends, family, and co-workers to engage in the study with you? You can access the sermons and small group session videos online at **ChurchoftheKing.com/PerspectiveShift**.

To best engage this study and truly have a *Perspective Shift* :

- Engage in weekend sermon messages.

- Engage in a small group.

- Engage in each of the daily devotionals and reflection questions.

FOR SMALL GROUP LEADERS

If you are leading or co-leading a small group, the section in the Appendix entitled Small Group Leader Orientation will give you valuable tips to encourage you and help you avoid common obstacles to effective small group leadership. Additional small group resources are available in the Appendices to help both small group leaders and participants. Please take some time to review these resources. Also, we've created several helpful videos and resources to complement this study guide. You can find those items at **ChurchoftheKing.com/PerspectiveShift.**

OUTLINE OF EACH SESSION

Each session for the *Perspective Shift* study in the book of Philippians includes the following sections:

Engage in the Sermon Messages

If you are also watching the weekly sermons that correspond to the themes of each session, feel free to use this page for personal notes and reflection.

Enjoy the Small Group Sessions

Connect with God and grow in community in a small group! This section provides everything you need for a group. Enjoy the weekly video sessions along with life-giving discussion questions that will encourage your group to open up and grow together.

Dive into the Daily Devotional Plan

Daily devotional guides have been written to help lead you on your *Perspective Shift* journey! Journal pages are included with each daily guide so you can reflect upon and write down what God is speaking to you. Note that each week's session includes six devotionals; the seventh day—called Weekly Reflection—is intended for a "reset" before beginning the next week's session. Each week, you find a key Bible verse for you to memorize. This memory verse will be focused on the topic of the week, and you can memorize a portion of the verse each day.

SESSION ONE

Happiness comes and goes with shifting circumstances. Joy is unshakeable, no matter how challenging our situations.

A JOYFUL LIFE

Paul teaches us something special about joy in his letter to the Philippians. He shows us that life is not just about the happy moments. We can experience deep joy – the kind that sticks around even during the tough times.

This week, let's think of joy in three ways:

1. People who feel joy only when things go right.

2. People who find joy every now and then.

3. People like the Apostle Paul, who have constant joy, no matter what happens.

Paul is a wonderful example of living with joy that we can all follow! His life shows us we can experience true joy through the power of Jesus Christ—even when the circumstances are overwhelming—even when the conflicts are painful. No matter what's happening on the outside, God can fill us with joy on the inside.

Weekend Message Notes And Questions

Use the following space to reflect on what you learned from the weekend message. Write down any questions you want to discuss with your small group.

_____

_____

_____

_____

_____

_____

_____

_____

_____

_____

_____

_____

_____

_____

SMALL GROUP A Joyful Life

Getting Started

Welcome to Session One! You and your small group are about to go on an amazing journey to experiencing joy in any circumstance! Let's start by getting to know each other.

- Share a little bit about yourself and what brought you to this small group.

- What do you hope to get out of the next six weeks?

Watch The Lesson

Each week, you will watch a session video together. You'll find space for notes, questions, and thoughts you want to share or remember. After watching the video, have someone read the lesson's discussion questions, then you can discuss them as a group. Remember to share the responsibilities of leading and reading each week.

SESSION 1 Video Notes

Philippians 2:5: _Let this mind be in you which was also in Christ Jesus._

The Differences between Joy and Happiness: *Happiness is fleeting, Joy is eternal*

Philippians 1:3-4: _I thank my God upon every remembrance of you, always in every prayer of mine making request for you all with joy,_

1. Happiness is **circumstantial** *____; joy is **relational** ____.

John 15:11: _"These things I have spoken to you, that My joy may remain in you, and that your joy may be full."_

Galatians 5:22-23: _But the fruit of the Spirit is love, joy, peace, longsuffering, kindness, goodness, faithfulness, gentleness, self-control. Against such there is no law._

2. Happiness is a **(destination) daily decision** ____; joy is a **daily decision** ____.

Philippians 1:6: _Being confident of this very thing, that He who has begun a good work in you will complete it until the day of Jesus Christ._ *You decide every day to walk in the joy of the Lord. The joy of the Lord will sustain you*

LET'S DISCUSS

In this section, we'll discuss how to practically apply the wisdom you have gained from the source material and Scriptures shared. We'll also explore actionable steps that can help you live out these principles.

1. This week's session defined the difference between happiness and joy. Share examples of times when you experienced happiness and times when you experienced joy.

Read Paul's words from **Philippians 1:6** as a group:

Being confident of this very thing, that He who has begun a good work in you will complete it until the day of Jesus Christ.

2. What does this verse tell us about God's commitment to our growth and journey?

3. How does understanding that God is continually working in us affect your perspective on daily challenges?

4. Can you recall a moment when you felt God was guiding you through a specific situation?

5. How can we ensure our daily choices align with pursuing God's plan for our lives?

Read **Nehemiah 8:10b** as a group:

   "...the joy of the LORD is your strength."

6. What does it mean to you that the joy of the Lord can be a source of strength in your life?

7. Why does our relationship with Christ impact our ability to experience genuine joy?

8. Give an example of a ~~time~~ that brought you temporary happiness but eventually left you feeling let down. What did you learn from that experience?

9. Share a time when you felt sustained by God's joy even in challenging circumstances.

10. What practical steps can you take to focus your life on Jesus and experience this joy consistently?

11. How can daily connection with God and other godly friends and family reinforce this joy in your life?

GO TO GOD

No matter the twists and turns of life, turning to God is always the right direction. He is the constant source of our joy, a wellspring that doesn't dry up with shifting circumstances. While happiness may ebb and flow, God's joy is eternal and unwavering.

Take time to:

1. Open up about the areas in your life where you find yourself chasing after fleeting happiness instead of the enduring joy of the Lord.

2. Intercede for others, noting down specific points so you can uphold them in prayer throughout the week.

3. Celebrate and share the joyous moments God's given you! What are you most grateful for today? Which prayers have you seen answered?

GET INTO ACTION

What are three tools or truths you took away from this session?

1. _____ Joy is a choice. _____

2. _____

3. We fight from a place of victory.

What is the main thing you believe God wants you to apply?

_____

_____

_____

_____

_____

_____

_____

_____

_____

_____

_____

_____

PRAYER AND PRAISE

Give each person a chance to share prayer requests and praise reports. Write your personal prayer requests and take notes on how you can pray for each other.

_____

_____

_____

_____

_____

_____

_____

_____

_____

_____

_____

_____

_____

_____

SESSION 1

DEVOTIONAL PLAN

DAY 1:

DON'T SETTLE FOR HAPPINESS

> ### ...And in this I rejoice, yes, and will rejoice...
> **PHILIPPIANS 1:18C**

Every now and then temporary moments of happiness touch our lives.

It might be a promotion, a surprise gift, or our favorite sports team winning the big game. These moments can be meaningful, but they come and go like waves on a beach. Joy, however, is something deeper. It's a life-giving river that flows from God's heart into yours, regardless of the storms that might rage outside.

The world can only offer temporary moments of happiness. but usually it's dependent on circumstances. One day you're up, the next you're down. In the book of Philippians, the Apostle Paul shows us an entirely different approach to life—a way of constant joy rooted in an unchanging God. To put this into perspective, you'll find the word "happy" only 22 times in the Bible, while "joy" appears 192 times!

Paul penned Philippians while under house arrest, chained to an elite Roman guard monitoring his every move. Yet, there isn't a hint of dissatisfaction, bitterness, or anger in his words. Paul's happiness was not dependent on his environment, but his joy was anchored in his relationship with Jesus. Even in extreme adversity, Paul emphasizes the good that's coming from his imprisonment. He doesn't say, "Rejoice when things are going well," but instead, "Rejoice in the Lord... always!"

So today, here's an invitation: don't settle for mere happiness when unshakable joy is yours in Christ.

REFLECT

Memory Verse

...Let this mind be in you which was also in Christ Jesus.
Philippians 2:5

To aid in your memorization, write out this week's memory verse:

_____

_____

How would you describe the difference between happiness and joy?

_____

_____

_____

What places in your life do you want that deep, never-ending joy? Ask God for it right now.

_____

_____

_____

Where do you habitually chase feelings of happiness rather than seeking God's joy?

_____

_____

_____

DAY 2:

JOY IN YOUR JOURNEY

> *Being confident of this very thing, that*
> *He who has begun a good work in you will*
> *complete it until the day of Jesus Christ.*
>
> **PHILIPPIANS 1:6**

Have you ever started a project and left it half-finished? We all have. But guess what? God never leaves His projects incomplete, especially with anything related to you.

In his letter, Paul is reassuring the Philippians—and us—that God is fully committed to our spiritual growth. God started a "good work" in you, and He will see it through to the end. His follow-through is perfect.

Here's what makes this journey so distinct. God's not conducting a cosmic self-help seminar to simply make us the "best version of ourselves." Instead, His "good work" in us is to make us more like *Christ*—which far exceeds anything we can do in our own effort.

Knowing this brings rest and peace to our soul that we're not doing life alone. The Creator of the Universe is actively shaping, guiding, and refining you. He's not a hobbyist, but the Master! He's in the business of creating masterpieces, fit for His glory.

So, why worry? Why let doubts, fears, and setbacks steal your joy? Trust in His plan. He's not done with you yet—and He always finishes what He starts! Find joy in the journey today, not just in the destination. If Paul did, we can too.

REFLECT

Memory Verse

...Let this mind be in you which was also in Christ Jesus.
Philippians 2:5

To aid in your memorization, write out this week's memory verse:

_____

_____

Do you sometimes feel like a "work in progress?" How does it feel to know God is committed to completing His work in you?

_____

_____

In what areas of your life have you experienced the most significant growth recently? In what areas do you feel like God wants you to grow?

_____

_____

How does the assurance of God's continual work in you affect your daily joy?

_____

_____

What's one way you can actively participate in God's "good work" in you today?

_____

_____

DAY 3:
GOLD MEDAL LIVES

> *Only let your conduct be worthy of the gospel of Christ, so that whether I come and see you or am absent, I may hear of your affairs, that you stand fast in one spirit, with one mind striving together for the faith of the gospel.*
>
> **PHILIPPIANS 1:27**

"There is strength in numbers." Most of us have probably used that statement or heard it said. But beyond strength in numbers, have you ever thought about the strength and joy that comes from being united in a common purpose? There is strength in power and unity.

Paul urges the Philippians to live "worthy of the gospel of Christ." But he doesn't stop there. He also stresses the importance of standing "fast in one spirit, with one mind." That's unity! Being united isn't just for fun nights singing around the campfire—but for a mission so grand it takes every one of us operating in our complementary gifts—the mission of the Gospel of Christ.

Paul put it this way in 1 Corinthians 12:12: *For as the body is one and has many members, but all the members of that one body, being many, are one body, so also is Christ.* Picture an athlete sprinting toward the finish line, going for the gold at the Olympics. What do you see? The runner's entire body "striving together" for the prize, though made of "many parts," moves in harmony toward a singular purpose.

This is how the Body of Christ operates when we all focus on Him! There is great joy knowing you're part of something vastly bigger than yourself—part of a community that's changing lives, uplifting spirits, and making a divine difference. When united in Christ, we don't just go through the motions of life. We live gold medal lives, worthy of the Gospel.

REFLECT

Memory Verse

...Let this mind be in you which was also in Christ Jesus.
Philippians 2:5

To aid in your memorization, write out this week's memory verse:

_____

_____

Where do you see opportunities for greater unity in your life?

_____

_____

How does unity in Christ differ from other types of unity you've experienced?

_____

_____

What specific steps can you take to foster unity in your community?

_____

_____

What would it look like for you to live a life "worthy of the gospel" today?

_____

_____

DAY 4:
THE JOY OF ENDURANCE

> ### *I press on toward the goal for the prize of the upward call of God in Christ Jesus.*
> **PHILIPPIANS 3:14**

Yesterday, we saw a picture of the Body of Christ represented by a gold medal athlete. Today, let's take it a little further. After all, an Olympian has more than raw strength—they have *endurance*.

Would you ever show up to the starting line of a marathon without having trained? I sure wouldn't! A life of faith is like a marathon—great joy comes from enduring and pressing on.

Just like Paul, who kept pressing "toward the goal," we're all in a spiritual marathon. There's a heavenly prize awaiting us, and to reach it, endurance is non-negotiable. Sometimes, the road will be smooth. We'll be running on a paved trail without a hill in sight. Other times, it'll feel like sprinting up a mountain. Yet Paul shows us there's a unique joy that comes from the grit it takes to develop godly endurance—and it isn't a fitness test you tackle on your own.

It's running with God's tailwind—a constant re-energizing from a source that's outside of yourself. In Colossians 1:29, Paul describes it as supernatural energy from God "which works in me mightily."

Endurance is far more than just our willpower and refusing to quit. It isn't about earning our place in God's family. It certainly isn't about impressing God or others. It's about drawing strength from God that doesn't make sense in the natural world; then letting that strength become your joy. If we're honest, could any of us build the endurance required to reach the "prize of the upward call of God" on our own? Not even close! Which is why Paul says he presses on "...in Christ Jesus." Yes, we're running a marathon that requires a great deal of endurance. But we don't manufacture the strength on our own. It comes from God with joy, power, and eternal satisfaction.

So my friend, how will you run today?

REFLECT

...Let this mind be in you which was also in Christ Jesus.
Philippians 2:5

To aid in your memorization, write out this week's memory verse:

_____

_____

What does the "upward call of God in Christ Jesus" mean to you personally?

_____

_____

Where in your life do you need more spiritual endurance?

_____

_____

How can you lean on God's strength when your own feels depleted?

_____

_____

What practical things can we do to have sustaining joy?

_____

_____

DAY 5:
THE JOY MINDSET

> *Let this mind be in you which was also in Christ Jesus.*
> **PHILIPPIANS 2:5**

The joy Paul wrote about, the joy he lived out, originated from his relationship with Christ. It dominated his mind and thought life, manifesting in his attitude, speech, and actions. It wasn't just how he felt, but how he thought. The same is true for us.

Your attitude affects your altitude. How you think affects how you feel. This letter to the Church of Philippi drives that point home—fifteen times, Paul writes about thinking, and ten times about remembering! Your mindset and your joy are inseparable.

This makes perfect sense when we consider a primary key to Christianity: you cannot change your heart, but you can change your mind. Conversely, God can change your heart, but He won't change your mind. So if I choose to change the way I think about a given situation, God will change my heart to follow suit. But, if I don't change my thoughts, God cannot change my heart. This is such an empowering truth.

Few people illustrate this truth better than Corrie ten Boom, a woman who found joy in excruciating circumstances in WWII. As the Holocaust raged, she and her family made the risky choice to help Jews evade the Nazis. The consequences of their bravery? Imprisonment. Even in that bleak place, she was able to say, "Joy runs deeper than despair." Not because of her surroundings, but because of where her mind and heart were anchored. If she could find joy in the midst of the Holocaust, surely we can tune our mind in to finding joy in our own daily challenges.

So, when Paul says in Philippians 2:5 to have the "mind of Christ," what's he really getting at? He was encouraging the Philippian believers to rejoice even in difficult circumstances. To respond and speak differently than expected. This flies in the face of today's world, doesn't it?

A joy mindset sees the bigger picture in the same way Jesus did. Between Paul's resilience and Corrie's spirit in the face of adversity, it's clear that joy's not about what's on the outside—it's an inside job!

REFLECT

Memory Verse

...Let this mind be in you which was also in Christ Jesus.
Philippians 2:5

To aid in your memorization, write out this week's memory verse:

_____

_____

Paul talks about having the "mind of Christ," emphasizing humility and selflessness. How can you practically apply these virtues in your daily life to cultivate a joy mindset?

_____

_____

_____

What challenges are you facing right now, and how can you anchor your mind and heart to find joy throughout the trials?

_____

_____

What are some external factors that you've allowed to negatively influence your joy, and how can you shift your focus inward to maintain a joyful spirit?

_____

_____

_____

...Let this mind be in you which was also in Christ Jesus.

Philippians 2:5

DAY 6:
WHAT STEALS YOUR JOY?

> *"Therefore you now have sorrow; but I will see you again and your heart will rejoice, and your joy no one will take from you."*
>
> JOHN 16:22

A businessman was once rushing to a meeting. Anxious and angry, he seemed to find every red light, detour, and delay in the city. Then, when he finally reached his destination, he realized he didn't have the keys to enter the building! But in the midst of his frustration, he remembered Jesus' promise in today's guiding verse—no one can steal our joy!

In today's verse, we see Jesus speaking with His disciples, preparing them for His death on the cross. While they didn't understand what He meant in the moment, they did after His resurrection. For God's people, sorrow can give way to true joy because it isn't dependent on circumstances or convenience. Joy is a fruit from the Holy Spirit—in both the *big* and *little* situations of life.

Real joy is rooted in Jesus Himself and is nurtured by the Holy Spirit. When we understand this, we see that our joy can remain untouched, regardless of external factors. The businessman's frustrating rush to a meeting is relatable and humorous, but what if that joy persisted in your life no matter how serious the situations you face?

Joy in a concerning diagnosis...
Joy amidst heartbreaking news from a friend...
Joy through a layoff that causes financial hardship...

You can have real, profound joy through it all. People around you will wonder, "How could you possibly face such a difficult situation with such joy?" You can answer with confidence: "Because Jesus said nothing can steal the joy that comes from knowing Him—not even this!"

REFLECT

...Let this mind be in you which was also in Christ Jesus.
Philippians 2:5

To aid in your memorization, write out this week's memory verse:

_____

_____

What situation is trying to steal your joy?

_____

_____

_____

How would a truly joy-filled person walk through that same situation? Can you emulate that?

_____

_____

_____

Take a moment to bring this situation before Jesus right now, asking for His joy in exchange for anxiety, anger, or heartbreak. Write down what you feel God speaks to you.

_____

_____

_____

WEEKLY REFLECTION

What are the top three realizations you had this session?

_____

_____

_____

_____

_____

_____

_____

What is the main thing you believe God wants you to apply?

_____

_____

_____

_____

_____

_____

_____

SESSION TWO

God doesn't call the strong to do the impossible; He strengthens the called to do the unimaginable.

SESSION 2 A Strong Life

Life can feel like an endless barrage of challenges, setbacks, and disappointments. Thankfully, the Apostle Paul's mindset and attitude provides us with a blueprint for enduring adversity. This week, we'll find four keys to lean into God's strength during tough times.

1. Be Positive: Because our God is good, there is always good to be found.

2. Stay Purposeful: Challenges are the very things that shape us, refine us, and point us to true north.

3. Maintain Perspective: The Bible calls life, with all its ups and downs, a vapor. Our home is in heaven, so we can live in light of eternity.

4. Remain Powerful: The Creator of the universe is on your side! So even when you feel weak, remember, His power is made perfect in your weakness.

No matter what you're facing this week, God's ready to share exactly what you need to build a strong life!

Weekend Message Notes And Questions

Use the following space to reflect on what you learned from the weekend message. Write down any questions you want to discuss with your small group.

_____

_____

_____

_____

_____

_____

_____

_____

_____

_____

_____

_____

_____

SMALL GROUP A Strong Life

Getting Started

Welcome to Session Two! Our goal is to shift our understanding and attitudes towards life's challenges and live from God's perspective. This week, we're going to find a supernatural source of strength. Let's start with these questions:

• Have you ever tried to look strong but ended up looking silly instead? Share.

• Have you ever felt overwhelmed by life's negative circumstances and thought about giving up?

Watch The Lesson

Next is a space for notes, questions, and thoughts you want to share or remember. After watching the video, have someone read the lesson's discussion questions, then you can discuss them as a group. Remember to share the responsibilities of leading and reading each week.

SESSION 2 Video Notes

John 16:33: *"These things I have spoken to you, that in Me you may have peace. In the world you will have tribulation; but be of good cheer, I have overcome the world."*

Three Ways to Respond to Adversity:

1. Be _____.

Philippians 1:12: *But I want you to know, brethren, that the things which happened to me have actually turned out for the furtherance of the gospel.*

2. Live _____.

Philippians 1:13-14: *So that it has become evident to the whole palace guard, and to all the rest, that my chains are in Christ; and most of the brethren in the Lord, having become confident by my chains, are much more bold to speak the word without fear.*

3. Maintain _____.

Philippians 1:19-21: *For I know that this will turn out for my deliverance through your prayer and the supply of the Spirit of Jesus Christ, according to my earnest expectation and hope that in nothing I shall be ashamed, but with all boldness, as always, so now also Christ will be magnified in my body, whether by life or by death. For to me, to live is Christ, and to die is gain.*

Answer key: positive, purposeful, perspective.

LET'S DISCUSS

In this section, talk about how you will apply the wisdom you have learned from the weekend message and small group study. Then discuss practical steps you can take to live out what you've learned.

Read **Philippians 1:12** as a group:

Now I want you to know, brothers and sisters, that what has happened to me has actually served to advance the gospel.

1. What does this verse reveal about Paul's attitude toward challenges?

2. How can we adopt a similar perspective, viewing our hardships as opportunities for growth and reaching others?

3. Have there been instances in your life where a difficult situation resulted in unexpected blessings or lessons?

4. Reflecting on Paul's experiences and teachings, how can we better align our focus on Christ rather than on our temporary discomforts and challenges?

5. How does our relationship with Jesus affect our view of negative circumstances?

Read **Philippians 1:19-21** as a group:

For I know that through your prayers and God's provision of the Spirit of Jesus Christ what has happened to me will turn out for my deliverance. I eagerly expect and hope that I will in no way be ashamed, but will have sufficient courage so that now as always Christ will be exalted in my body, whether by life or by death. For to me, to live is Christ and to die is gain.

6. Discuss the concept of "To live is Christ..." How does this statement apply to our daily choices, actions, and attitudes?

7. How does Paul's perspective on life and death challenge our way of thinking?

8. How can we shift our minds to make choices based on the eternal instead of the temporary?

GET INTO ACTION

What are three tools or truths you took away from this session?

1. _____

2. _____

3. _____

What is the main thing you believe God wants you to apply?

_____

_____

_____

_____

_____

_____

_____

_____

_____

_____

_____

_____

GO TO GOD

Our world is ever-changing, but God remains our unchanging anchor. Embracing His eternal perspective can transform our fleeting frustrations into lasting lessons.

During this time:

1. Open up about the areas in your life where you've felt overwhelmed by challenges, seeking the group's support and prayers.

2. Intercede for those facing adversity, keeping specific prayer requests in mind to uphold them throughout the week.

3. Celebrate the victories, both big and small, that God has brought into your life. What instances remind you of God's unwavering love and faithfulness?

PRAYER AND PRAISE

Give each person a chance to share prayer requests and praise reports. Write your personal prayer requests and take notes on how you can pray for each other.

_____

_____

_____

_____

_____

_____

_____

_____

_____

_____

_____

_____

_____

_____

SESSION 2

DEVOTIONAL PLAN

DAY 8:
ACORNS INTO OAK TREES

But I want you to know, brethren, that the things which happened to me have actually turned out for the furtherance of the gospel, so that it has become evident to the whole palace guard, and to all the rest, that my chains are in Christ;
PHILIPPIANS 1:12-13

Imagine an acorn. It's first planted in complete darkness. Then, in time, it sprouts roots to access the water in the soil and a shoot that stretches to the sun. This small seed buried in the ground becomes *exceptionally different* and *radically better*.

Even the mightiest of oaks start in a dark place in order to grow into God's grand design. In a similar way, our hard times can feel like the soil. You question,"Why am I here in this place?" But God can use those difficult places of darkness and isolation to grow into something more wonderful than we ever thought possible.

Paul's imprisonment was similar "soil." His seemingly awful situation "actually turned out for the furtherance of the gospel." What seemed buried, done for, and gone for good was just getting started. When Paul shared the Gospel, he planted a "seed" in someone's heart. Jesus explained in Matthew 13:23 that everyone who heard and understood the Gospel had a heart made of "good soil." Good soil produces new life!

Paul experienced great difficulties in his life. It was in prison, he wrote this letter to the Philippians that millions have been encouraged by for two thousand years. The beauty is, God uses the seemingly irredeemable to grow abundant life. He does the same for us today. He turns our hard times into moments of victory.

Finding joy in dark times starts with a perspective shift. Like Paul, we can zoom out and see He's still turning acorns into oak trees. He can do the same in your life right *now*.

REFLECT

For to me, to live is Christ, and to die is gain. **Philippians 1:21**

To aid in your memorization, write out this week's memory verse:

_____

_____

Have there been moments in your life where unexpected joy or growth sprouted from difficult circumstances? Describe one.

_____

_____

In what areas of your life might you need a perspective shift to see God's purpose at work, even amidst challenges?

_____

_____

How can you embrace the concept that, like Paul, your hardships might "actually serve to advance the gospel" in your own life or the lives of others?

_____

_____

What practical steps can you take to seek joy and purpose when facing trying times, just as Paul did?

_____

_____

DAY 9:
LIVE WITH ETERNAL PERSPECTIVE

> *For I am hard-pressed between the two, having a desire to depart and be with Christ, which is far better. Nevertheless to remain in the flesh is more needful for you.*
> **PHILIPPIANS 1:23-24**

The tug-of-war of life often leaves us caught between our earthly realities and the promise of an eternal home. I frequently find myself thinking about heaven, especially during those moments when life feels overwhelming. It's comforting to imagine a place with no sorrow, pain, or tears—a place where all things are made new.

In Philippians, Paul shares his own tug-of-war. He feels the pull toward heaven with "a desire to depart and be with Jesus." Yet, he knows there's work left to be done on Earth. For Paul, it's not about escaping troubles but understanding the bigger picture.

When we remember that our stay here is temporary, our current struggles feel lighter. Our problems, no matter how large, become blips on the radar of eternity.

Like looking out across a landscape from a mountaintop, an eternal perspective helps us see life's challenges in their true scale. It reminds us that every heartache, every struggle, and every pain has an expiration date. This doesn't make our trials insignificant, yet it certainly changes how we respond to them.

Set your sights on the eternal, knowing that this world is not your home. As Paul shared in 2 Corinthians 4:17: *For our light affliction, which is but for a moment, is working for us a far more exceeding and eternal weight of glory.*

What is coming far outweighs what is happening now. Today, make the decision to live with an eternal perspective, which is "far better."

REFLECT

Memory Verse

For to me, to live is Christ, and to die is gain. **Philippians 1:21**

To aid in your memorization, write out this week's memory verse:

_____

_____

How does having an eternal perspective influence your daily decisions?

_____

_____

What aspects of your life need a heavenly perspective?

_____

_____

How does focusing on heaven bring comfort during trying times?

_____

_____

In what ways can you remind yourself of the eternal when faced with the temporal?

_____

_____

_____

DAY 10:
PROGRESS AND JOY

And being confident of this, I know that
I shall remain and continue with you all
for your progress and joy of faith.

PHILIPPIANS 1:25

Charles Haddon Spurgeon is a well-known and famous 19th century British preacher. However, not many people know much of his wife, Susannah. Early in their marriage, she became so sick she could barely leave their house. But she felt a strong need to do something more for their ministry. She decided to help pastors who couldn't afford her husband's books. So, from the confines of her home she started a program called the "Book Fund". Susannah's "Book Fund" gave thousands of pastors the books and resources they needed to advance God's mission in their own ministries.

Susannah was a trailblazer, and a perfect illustration of the "progress" Paul speaks about in today's guiding verse. His aim was directed toward the Philippians' progress and joy in faith.

The Greek word for *progress* here (prokopé) isn't defined as a meandering trudge along an ambiguous path. Instead, it means more like cutting a direct path through dense forest and underbrush to advance a marching army.

Paul knew the Philippians were called to be pioneers for the Gospel. They were persevering through persecution. They were coming against demonic opposition. They were sharing the hope of the Gospel! What was the outcome of that pioneering progress? Joy.

Making progress in our faith, both in our character and our actions, produces joy. So try this—the next time joy seems to be eluding you, ask the Holy Spirit for a perspective shift—to show you the next step in your "progress...of faith." Then, take the step in faith—joy will most certainly follow.

REFLECT

For to me, to live is Christ, and to die is gain. **Philippians 1:21**

To aid in your memorization, write out this week's memory verse:

_____

_____

In what ways are you currently pioneering or "cutting a path" in your faith journey? Are there obstacles or "underbrush" that you need to clear to advance?

_____

_____

_____

Like Susannah Spurgeon, what limitations or challenges are you facing right now that could actually be avenues for progress and joy in your faith?

_____

_____

_____

What is the next step in your "progress...of faith," and how can you take it to experience joy?

_____

_____

DAY 11:
BUILDING SPIRITUAL STRENGTH

> *"These things I have spoken to you, that in Me you may have peace. In the world you will have tribulation; but be of good cheer, I have overcome the world."*
> JOHN 16:33

In both the gym and life, progress typically comes through pressure. How is that for a perspective shift? At the gym, you lift weights or run to build physical strength. Similarly, in our spiritual lives, we face various forms of pressure—job stress, relationship issues, and other life challenges. The key in all life scenarios is how we respond. Just as the improper lifting of weights can cause injury, responding poorly to life's pressures can set us back.

It's important to understand that adversity is not a sign of divine punishment; it's a part of life Jesus guaranteed would come! He said in the world we'll have *tribulation*, or difficult trials. Adversity will come. Just like Jesus, Paul went through many trials and temptations. But he didn't give in to them—he stood firm. As a result, when he allowed God to work through them his life became a powerful testimony to the grace of God.

Pressure builds strength! But it also reveals.

So, why do we face trials? They serve as spiritual workouts, producing pressure that can reveal wrong attitudes and impure motives. When we address these issues, we grow stronger in our faith. In essence, it's not the trials themselves, but it's our response that leads us to spiritual growth.

Just as you wouldn't avoid lifting weights or going for a run to build strength, don't shy away from life's challenges. They are opportunities for spiritual growth.

REFLECT

Memory Verse

For to me, to live is Christ, and to die is gain. **Philippians 1:21**

To aid in your memorization, write out this week's memory verse:

_____

_____

Reflect on a recent challenge or pressure you've faced. How did you respond, and what did it reveal about your spiritual strength or areas for growth?

_____

_____

_____

Read John 16:33. How does this promise affect your perspective on the trials you're currently experiencing?

_____

_____

_____

What practical steps can you take to respond to life's pressures in a way that strengthens your faith this week?

_____

_____

_____

DAY 12:
STRENGTH IN WEAKNESS

> *Concerning this thing I pleaded with the Lord three times that it might depart from me. And He said to me, "My grace is sufficient for you, for My strength is made perfect in weakness..."*
>
> 2 CORINTHIANS 12:8-9A

Do you ever feel like adversity seems to follow you? You may find it counterintuitive, but accepting our weakness can lead to our greatest strength. Sounds like a paradox, right? But this is precisely what we see in Paul's life.

In today's guiding verse, Paul "pleaded" for the Lord to remove what he called a "thorn" in his flesh. While we don't know exactly what it was, we do know that it was a serious challenge for Paul. Yet, Jesus's answer wasn't what he'd expected. *My grace is sufficient for you, for My strength is made perfect in weakness."* Talk about a perspective shift!

In this, Paul learned that no matter how strong or problem-free we seem, none of us has the power to walk the Christian life in our own power.

In our culture of self-reliance, we're told to power through, to be strong, and to embrace independence. The reality is, we all have cracks and limitations in our lives where we don't feel quite as sturdy? God specializes in filling those very gaps. He doesn't just want to make us stronger; He wants to be our Source of strength.

So today, don't shy away from your adversities. Embrace them, because in doing so, you're opening doors for God to work in miraculous ways. "His strength is made perfect in our weakness."

REFLECT

Memory Verse

For to me, to live is Christ, and to die is gain. **Philippians 1:21**

To aid in your memorization, write out this week's memory verse:

_____

_____

What are some weaknesses you've been hesitant to embrace?

_____

_____

How can your weaknesses become a testament to God's power in your life?

_____

_____

Are you relying on your own strength or inviting God to fill in your gaps?

_____

_____

How can embracing weakness lead to a deeper relationship with God?

_____

_____

DAY 13:
TURN BARRIERS INTO BRIDGES

But I want you to know, brethren, that the things which happened to me have actually turned out for the furtherance of the gospel, so that it has become evident to the whole palace guard, and to all the rest, that my chains are in Christ; and most of the brethren in the Lord, having become confident by my chains, are much more bold to speak the word without fear.

PHILIPPIANS 1:12-14

When life puts you in chains, where do you see yourself: trapped in a prison cell or in the center of a new opportunity? Let's talk about Paul's perspective.

Paul was under surveillance and imprisonment by the infamous and elite Praetorian Guard. They were special forces like the Navy Seals or Green Berets. They were the elite of the elite, responsible for protecting Roman emperors.

To most, they would mean it's the end of the road. But Paul? He saw an audience. He discerned the deeper opportunity. He was physically chained, but his spirit was unbound and free. Rather than seeing the Praetorian Guard as his jailers, he saw people who desperately needed the Gospel.

Our circumstances can be hard—even grave. But Paul shows us that opportunities can lie behind our obstacles and circumstances. It's not about ignoring reality but understanding God's deeper purpose behind it. So what if your challenge, your "prison," is the gateway to impacting people you'd never imagined you could reach? Can you say, like Paul, "My chains are in Christ"?

Sometimes, the things we see as barriers are bridges to God's purpose for our lives. Today, shift your perspective to match His and watch it turn out "for the furtherance of the Gospel."

REFLECT

For to me, to live is Christ, and to die is gain. **Philippians 1:21**

To aid in your memorization, write out this week's memory verse:

_____

_____

Which areas of your life have felt restrictive lately? What might be the hidden opportunity within them?

_____

_____

_____

Considering Paul's perspective with the Praetorian Guard, how can you shift your view of current trials?

_____

_____

_____

Think about a recent challenge. How might that situation serve a greater purpose than you initially thought?

_____

_____

_____

WEEKLY REFLECTION

What are the top three realizations you had this session?

_____

_____

_____

_____

_____

_____

What is the main thing you believe God wants you to apply?

_____

_____

_____

_____

_____

_____

SESSION THREE

Jesus doesn't just see us as we are today, He sees us as who He made us to become.

SESSION 3 A Humble Life

Have you ever thought about how Jesus lived His life? He was always helping, healing, and encouraging those around Him. He was humble and overflowing with compassion. His mind was filled with wisdom, and His hands were always ready to serve.

This week, we'll discover together how to have a heart like Jesus, think with His wisdom, and serve with hands that genuinely care. I call it becoming a Dream Releaser, and it looks like this:

1. The Heart of a Dream Releaser: A heart full of compassion and selfless love, always seeking to empathize and uplift those around.

2. The Head of a Dream Releaser: A mindset anchored in wisdom and the Bible's teachings, valuing everyone's worth, including their own.

3. The Hands of a Dream Releaser: Hands that put heart's intent and head's wisdom into tangible action, always reaching out to help and heal.

It's time to follow in Jesus' footsteps along a path of genuine humility, compassionate service, and releasing dreams!

Weekend Message Notes And Questions

Use the following space to reflect on what you learned from the weekend message. Write down any questions you want to discuss with your small group.

_____

_____

_____

_____

_____

_____

_____

_____

_____

_____

_____

_____

_____

_____

SMALL GROUP A Humble Life

Getting Started

Welcome to Week Three! This week, we're doing the work of setting aside our pride and embracing the way of Jesus: humility and service. These aren't easy (or natural) things to do. But the right perspective shows us how.

Let's start our journey with some reflection:

• What does humility mean to you?

• Share a time when you saw true humility in someone's life. How did it impact you or others?

Watch The Lesson

Next is a space for notes, questions, and thoughts you want to share or remember. After watching the video, have someone read the lesson's discussion questions, then you can discuss them as a group. Remember to share the responsibilities of leading and reading each week.

Humility: Freedom from pride and arrogance.

Mark 10:45: *"For even the Son of Man did not come to be served, but to serve, and to give His life a ransom for many."*

Acts 26:15-16: *"So I said, 'Who are You, Lord?' And He said, 'I am Jesus, whom you are persecuting. But rise and stand on your feet; for I have appeared to you for this purpose, to make you a minister and a witness both of the things which you have seen and of the things which I will yet reveal to you."*

Three Characteristics of a Dream Releaser:

1. The _____ of a Dream Releaser.

Philippians 2:1-4: *Therefore if there is any consolation in Christ, if any comfort of love, if any fellowship of the Spirit, if any affection and mercy, fulfill my joy by being like-minded, having the same love, being of one accord, of one mind. Let nothing be done through selfish ambition or conceit, but in lowliness of mind let each esteem others better than himself. Let each of you look out not only for his own interests, but also for the interests of others.*

2. The _____ of a Dream Releaser.

Philippians 2:5: *Let this mind be in you which was also in Christ Jesus.*

Romans 8:32: *He who did not spare His own Son, but delivered Him up for us all, how shall He not with Him also freely give us all things?*

2 Corinthians 4:7: *But we have this treasure in earthen vessels, that the excellence of the power may be of God and not of us.*

3. The _____ of a Dream Releaser.

Philippians 2:7-8: *But made Himself of no reputation, taking the form of a bondservant, and coming in the likeness of men. And being found in appearance as a man, He humbled Himself and became obedient to the point of death, even the death of the cross.*

John 13:3-5: *Jesus, knowing that the Father had given all things into His hands, and that He had come from God and was going to God, rose from supper and laid aside His garments, took a towel and girded Himself. After that, He poured water into a basin and began to wash the disciples' feet, and to wipe them with the towel with which He was girded.*

Answer key: heart, head, hands

LET'S DISCUSS

In this section, talk about how you will apply the wisdom you have learned from the weekend message and small group study. Then discuss practical steps you can take to live out what you've learned.

Read **Philippians 2:7-8** as a group:

...but made Himself of no reputation, taking the form of a bondservant, and coming in the likeness of men. And being found in appearance as a man, He humbled Himself and became obedient to the point of death, even the death of the cross.

1. Discuss the difference between the world's view and God's view of humility.

2. What is the relationship between humility and servant leadership?

3. How does this verse depict Jesus' humility?

4. How can we model Jesus' servant leadership in our daily lives?

5. Can you think of someone who has been a Dream Releaser–or servant leader–in your life?

6. What are some practical ways we can humble ourselves?

7. What steps can we take to nurture and recognize the potential in others around us?

Read **John 13:3-5** as a group:

Jesus, knowing that the Father had given all things into His hands, and that He had come from God and was going to God, rose from supper and laid aside His garments, took a towel and girded Himself. After that, He poured water into a basin and began to wash the disciples' feet, and to wipe them with the towel with which He was girded.

8. Why do you think Jesus chose to wash the disciples' feet, and what does this action signify?

9. How does Jesus' act of service challenge our understanding of leadership and greatness in the kingdom of God?

10. Share a time when a leader in your life served you.

11. Have there been moments in your life where you've been called to humble yourself and serve others, even when you felt it was below your status or comfort zone?

12. How can we emulate Jesus' example of servant leadership in our daily lives and interactions with others?

13. What barriers or mindset shifts need to occur for us to genuinely serve and uplift others, even when it might not benefit us directly?

GO TO GOD

As we go through life, we should aim to be humble and help others achieve their dreams. Jesus showed us the way by serving others, even dying on the cross for us. His desire to be a Dream Releaser should be our guide.

Take a moment to:

1. Reflect on areas where you might need a perspective shift towards humility.

2. Pray for those in your life who need someone to believe in them, to release their dreams.

3. Share a testimony or story where someone played a pivotal role in realizing your dreams or potential. Who has been a Dream Releaser for you?

GET INTO ACTION

What are three tools or truths you took away from this session?

1. _____

2. _____

3. _____

What is the main thing you believe God wants you to apply?

_____

_____

_____

_____

_____

_____

_____

_____

_____

_____

_____

_____

PRAYER AND PRAISE

Give each person a chance to share prayer requests and praise reports. Write your personal prayer requests and take notes on how you can pray for each other.

_____

_____

_____

_____

_____

_____

_____

_____

_____

_____

_____

_____

_____

_____

SESSION 3

DEVOTIONAL PLAN

DAY 15:
EVERYONE NEEDS A DREAM RELEASER

> *And when Saul had come to Jerusalem, he tried to join the disciples; but they were all afraid of him, and did not believe that he was a disciple. But Barnabas took him and brought him to the apostles. And he declared to them how he had seen the Lord on the road, and that He had spoken to him, and how he had preached boldly at Damascus in the name of Jesus.*
>
> ACTS 9:26-27

Of all the writings in the New Testament, Paul wrote the most. That's quite a legacy. But did you know his journey with Jesus didn't start in a very promising way?

Today's verses share what happened after Paul (still called Saul at that point) had a life-changing experience with Jesus. He was changed dramatically–transformed from a fierce enemy of the cross to a joyful evangelist. However, the disciples didn't believe the man who had been persecuting their fellow Christians was genuine. Instead, they thought it was a ploy to win their trust and take them down from the inside.

How could Paul possibly overcome an obstacle like this? Well, Paul had a Dream Releaser named Barnabas in his life. A Dream Releaser is a true servant leader. Dream Releasers love, care for, and help others achieve the dreams God placed inside of them. Barnabas was a Dream Releaser who didn't look at people at face value. Dream Releasers see others through God's eyes, envisioning their full potential, encouraging them, and even becoming their champion.

After Barnabas served as a Dream Releaser for him, we see Paul become the same for many around him. Paul made it a habit and priority to help others discover the dream, purpose, and desires God put in their hearts.

While the disciples were leery of Paul at the beginning, the Philippian believers deeply trusted him—even from a distance. Why? Because Paul, like Barnabas, was a Dream Releaser for them!

Today, God wants us to become the same: true servant leaders who change the course of peoples' lives. Are you ready?

REFLECT:

Let nothing be done through selfish ambition or conceit, but in lowliness of mind let each esteem others better than himself. Let each of you look out not only for his own interests, but also for the interests of others.
Philippians 2:3-4

To aid in your memorization, write out this week's memory verse:

_____

_____

_____

_____

Who has been a Dream Releaser in your life?

_____

_____

_____

_____

What did they say or do for you that made a real impact?

_____

_____

_____

_____

When have you been a Dream Releaser for others?

_____

_____

_____

_____

Who is God calling you to serve in this way right now? What can you do to be a Dream Releaser for them?

_____

_____

_____

_____

DAY 16:
WHAT DOES JESUS SEE IN YOU?

"For even the Son of Man did not come to be served, but to serve, and to give His life a ransom for many."
MARK 10:45

Have you ever wondered what Jesus sees when He looks at you? Could it be possible that He sees not just who you are now, but who you can become?

In Mark 10:45, Jesus declares His mission—to serve others and give His life as a ransom for many. He was the ultimate Dream Releaser... the consummate servant leader. He saw the potential in people. He saw fishermen by the Sea of Galilee and envisioned them as world-changers and carriers of the Good News.

We learned yesterday Jesus saw Paul for his potential, not for his past. Before his conversion, Paul was a persecutor, even a murderer, bent on destroying the Church (Acts 8:3). Now, let's dig a little deeper into what actually happened when Paul met Jesus for the first time. Acts 9:1–4 tells us:

Then Saul, still breathing threats and murder against the disciples of the Lord, went to the high priest and asked letters from him to the synagogues of Damascus, so that if he found any who were of the Way, whether men or women, he might bring them bound to Jerusalem. As he journeyed he came near Damascus, and suddenly a light shone around him from heaven. Then he fell to the ground, and heard a voice saying to him, "Saul, Saul, why are you persecuting Me?"

Later, Paul in Acts 26:16 shared what else Jesus told him that day:

> *"But rise and stand on your feet; for I have appeared to you for this purpose, to make you a minister and a witness..."*

Isn't that powerful? Jesus saw beyond Paul's rage. He saw a future apostle, a future Dream Releaser. Just like Paul, you too have been touched by the Master Dream Releaser. Jesus sees beyond your flaws, your past mistakes, and your current circumstances and limitations. He sees the incredible potential within you waiting to be unlocked. After all, He put it there!

REFLECT:

Memory Verse

Let nothing be done through selfish ambition or conceit, but in lowliness of mind let each esteem others better than himself. Let each of you look out not only for his own interests, but also for the interests of others.
Philippians 2:3-4

To aid in your memorization, write out this week's memory verse:

_____

_____

_____

_____

What mask are you wearing that you think Jesus can't see beyond?

_____

_____

_____

_____

What dream has God placed in your heart?

_____

_____

_____

_____

Are you ready for Jesus to release your dream? If so, ask Him right now.

_____

_____

_____

_____

How can you serve others this week in a way that reflects Jesus' mission in Mark 10:45?

_____

_____

_____

_____

DAY 17:
HEART OF A DREAM RELEASER

> *Therefore if there is any consolation in Christ, if any comfort of love, if any fellowship of the Spirit, if any affection and mercy, fulfill my joy by being like-minded, having the same love, being of one accord, of one mind. Let nothing be done through selfish ambition or conceit, but in lowliness of mind let each esteem others better than himself. Let each of you look out not only for his own interests, but also for the interests of others.*
>
> **PHILIPPIANS 2:1-4**

When I was in Bible school—lonely and far from home—a family noticed me and invited me to dinner. They were warm, loving, encouraging, and made me feel like a part of their family. They invested in me because they believed in me!

They were Dream Releasers.

Today's guiding verses perfectly outline the traits that make up the heart of a Dream Releaser—encouragement, love, affection, and mercy. These traits create a "Greenhouse Effect," they create an environment where dreams can flourish. Just like a plant needs the right conditions to grow, people need unconditional love, compassion, and encouragement to see their dreams released.

Jesus was the epitome of love and compassion. In Matthew 14:14, we read that Jesus was "...moved with compassion for them, and healed their sick." He didn't just feel sorry for them; His compassion moved Him to action. Likewise, as His disciples, let's be moved by compassion to help others. Compassion compels us to invest our time, money, and effort into the lives of those in need.

When you see someone struggling, whether emotionally or financially, go beyond commenting on their social media posts. Take the time to show genuine concern. Ask yourself, "What would Jesus do in this situation?" Remember, unending joy is found in the way of Jesus. So my friend, let's walk as He walked.

REFLECT

Memory Verse

Let nothing be done through selfish ambition or conceit, but in lowliness of mind let each esteem others better than himself. Let each of you look out not only for his own interests, but also for the interests of others.
Philippians 2:3-4

To aid in your memorization, write out this week's memory verse:

_____

_____

_____

_____

What traits of a Dream Releaser do you already possess, and which do you need to develop?

_____

_____

How can you create a "greenhouse effect" for someone's dreams to flourish?

_____

_____

What specific action can you take today to show compassion to someone in need?

_____

_____

DAY 18:
HEAD OF A DREAM RELEASER

> *Let this mind be in you which was also in Christ Jesus.*
> **PHILIPPIANS 2:5**

Years ago, I worked with a young man at a restaurant who thought the best way to build his self-esteem was to tear others' self-esteem down. He couldn't have been more wrong. True self-worth comes from lifting others up, not tearing them down.

The mindset of a Dream Releaser is as crucial as the heart. Philippians 2:5 urges us to adopt the same mindset as Christ. This mindset is not just about how we feel but also about how we think—about ourselves, others, and God.

First, our thoughts about ourselves must be balanced. True humility doesn't mean devaluing ourselves; it means esteeming others without losing sight of our own worth. Romans 12:3 advises us to think soberly about ourselves, neither inflating nor deflating our self-worth.

Second, our thoughts about others must be correct. We must look past human frailties to see the fingerprint of God upon each person.

Last, our thoughts about God must be accurate. If we view God as stingy or limited, we'll walk in fear and comparison. Yet Romans 8:32 reminds us that God is the God of "more than enough." He freely gives us all things. God's nature is abundant.

So, how do we cultivate this mindset? By renewing our minds through Scripture. As we study and encounter God in the Bible, we learn to see ourselves and others through His eyes.

REFLECT

Memory Verse

Let nothing be done through selfish ambition or conceit, but in lowliness of mind let each esteem others better than himself. Let each of you look out not only for his own interests, but also for the interests of others.
Philippians 2:3-4

To aid in your memorization, write out this week's memory verse:

_____

_____

_____

_____

How does your current mindset align or conflict with the mindset of a Dream Releaser?

_____

_____

What steps can you take to align your thoughts about God, others, and yourself with Scripture?

_____

_____

Can you recall a time when renewing your thoughts led to a change in your actions?

_____

_____

DAY 19:
HANDS OF A DREAM RELEASER

> *But made Himself of no reputation, taking the form of a bondservant, and coming in the likeness of men. And being found in appearance as a man, He humbled Himself and became obedient to the point of death, even the death of the cross.*
> **PHILIPPIANS 2:7-8**

Imagine trading a throne for a manger, and heavenly glory for earthly humility. That's exactly what Jesus did to extend His hands to you and me.

Philippians 2:7-8 paints a vivid picture of Jesus' humility and servitude. He left the comfort and glory of heaven to become a servant on Earth. He traded a world of perfection for one of imperfection. He traded everything to extend His hands to humanity. That's true humility and love.

Jesus didn't just talk about servitude–He lived it. In John 13:3-5, we see Him washing the disciples' feet—an act reserved for only the lowest of servants. Even though He was fully aware of His divine identity, He chose to pick up a towel and wash grimy, dirty feet. His hands, soon to be pierced, served others until the end.

Jesus took the place of servanthood. He was the ultimate Servant Leader. He looked past Peter's impulsiveness and Paul's rage, loving them and believing the best in them. He released them into their dreams, even at great personal cost. Jesus carried this commitment all the way to the cross, enduring pain and suffering for our sake. Sometimes, being a Dream Releaser is inconvenient and even painful. Where do you need to pick up a towel to serve and love others? Being a dream releaser is a cost worth paying.

Are you willing to extend your hands to help others–even if it costs you? Are you willing to make yourself "of no reputation"? Jesus did it for you–can you do it for someone else?

REFLECT

Let nothing be done through selfish ambition or conceit, but in lowliness of mind let each esteem others better than himself. Let each of you look out not only for his own interests, but also for the interests of others.
Philippians 2:3-4

To aid in your memorization, write out this week's memory verse:

_____

_____

_____

_____

How have you extended your hand to help others in the past?

_____

_____

Who has God put on your heart to help develop right now?

_____

_____

What personal sacrifices might you have to make to become a Dream Releaser for him or her?

_____

How can you practically help that person grow and reach their God-given potential?

_____

DAY 20:
SEEING GOD AS HE IS

> *He who did not spare His own Son, but delivered Him up for us all, how shall He not with Him also freely give us all things?*
>
> ROMANS 8:32

When you imagine God, what is He like? What does He care about? Is He interested in your life? Is He angry with you? Is He a limitless provider or a stingy gatekeeper?

Scripture reveals a God of abundance, the God of "more than enough." He's a God Who wants to fulfill the desires He placed in your heart (Psalm 37:4). However, if you don't see God from a biblical perspective, every area of your life can suffer. Instead of seeing God as *He is*, you get stuck trying to follow God as *He's not*.

Think of it like this. What if you believed touching a hot stove saves your hand from getting burned while cooking? I know... it's ludicrous! But in the same way, believing lies creates very painful problems! Your beliefs shape your thoughts and your thoughts become actions.

How you view God determines how you pursue Him. If you believe He's uninterested in you, would you spend time with Him? Probably not. If you think He's always angry or disappointed, would you do "good things" to earn His love? Probably not. But if you knew He loves you and is deeply interested in you, you would quickly shift your perspective.

I've found that going to Scripture directly is the most powerful way to see God as He really is—loving, compassionate, protective, generous, and more! Today's guiding verse tells us that His generosity was so extravagant that He traded Jesus' life for ours. Also, His deep desire is "to freely give us all things."

Now, take a few moments to read the following verses and then write down the perspective each gives us on what God is really like.

Matthew 7:11	
2 Corinthians 9:8	
Psalm 84:11	
Lamentations 3:22-23	
Philippians 4:19	

REFLECT

Let nothing be done through selfish ambition or conceit, but in lowliness of mind let each esteem others better than himself. Let each of you look out not only for his own interests, but also for the interests of others.
Philippians 2:3-4

To aid in your memorization, write out this week's memory verse:

_____

_____

_____

_____

What attribute of God's character stood out to you most? Why?

_____

_____

Where do you need to replace lies about God with truth?

_____

_____

Connect the dots between *believing right* with *living right*. Jot down or share a story with someone else that shows how your beliefs drove positive, or negative, actions.

_____

_____

WEEKLY REFLECTION

What are the top three realizations you had this session?

_____

_____

_____

_____

_____

_____

What is the main thing you believe God wants you to apply?

_____

_____

_____

_____

_____

_____

SESSION FOUR

Focus helps us pursue God's best over distractions, diversions, and dead-ends.

SESSION 4 A Focused Life

Paul's life is one of unwavering faith and perseverance. Despite being a prisoner of Rome with a painful past, he never slowed down. He never stayed silent.

Paul was a man on a grand mission—and this week, we'll tap into the secret of his endurance and fortitude. We're meant to do what he did—to run, to grow, and to win in life by focusing on Christ.

We'll do this by tackling three things:

1. Letting go of past mistakes.

2. Embracing today.

3. Aiming for a brighter future with God.

Like Paul, we'll find endless strength in Christ if we don't lose focus.

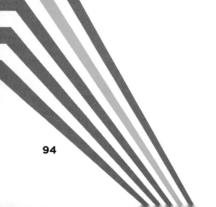

Weekend Message Notes And Questions

Use the following space to reflect on what you learned from the weekend message. Write down any questions you want to discuss with your small group.

_____

_____

_____

_____

_____

_____

_____

_____

_____

_____

_____

_____

_____

SMALL GROUP A Focused Life

Getting Started

Intentionality is more than just wanting to win. It's about understanding your unique God-given purpose, and fulfilling it! Let's start Week Four by answering these questions:

- How do you define intentionality in your life?

- What barriers or past pains hinder you from living with focus and passion?

Watch The Lesson

Next is a space for notes, questions, and thoughts you want to share or remember. After watching the video, have someone read the lesson's discussion questions, then you can discuss them as a group. Remember to share the responsibilities of leading and reading each week.

Philippians 3:13-14: *Brethren, I do not count myself to have apprehended; but one thing I do, forgetting those things which are behind and reaching forward to those things which are ahead, I press toward the goal for the prize of the upward call of God in Christ Jesus.*

1 Corinthians 9:24-26 (NLT): *Don't you realize that in a race everyone runs, but only one person gets the prize? So run to win! All athletes are disciplined in their training. They do it to win a prize that will fade away, but we do it for an eternal prize. So I run with purpose in every step. I am not just shadowboxing.*

Philippians 3:13: *...those things which are behind...*

1. Run with a _____.

Philippians 3:14: *I press toward the goal for the prize of the upward call of God in Christ Jesus.*

Proverbs 4:25-27 (NIV): *Let your eyes look straight ahead; fix your gaze directly before you. Give careful thought to the paths for your feet and be steadfast in all your ways. Do not turn to the right or the left; keep your foot from evil.*

2. Run with a _____.

Living Forward by Michael Hyatt and Daniel Harkavy.

3. Run with _____.

Philippians 3:17: *Brethren, join in following my example, and note those who so walk, as you have us for a pattern.*

Hebrews 10:24-25 (NIV):*And let us consider how we may spur one another on toward love and good deeds, not giving up meeting together, as some are in the habit of doing, but encouraging one another...*

Answer key: goal, plan, people

LET'S DISCUSS

Reflect on Paul's life, his challenges, victories, and his drive for intentional living.

Read **Philippians 3:13-14** as a group:

...those things which are behind... need to be left in the past... I press toward the goal for the prize of the upward call of God in Christ Jesus.

1. What goals have God set before you, and how are you pressing toward them?

2. How does Paul's perspective on running the race inspire you in your personal journey?

3. What steps can you take to be more intentional and purpose-driven in your life?

4. How can leaving the past behind pave the way for a brighter future?

5. What are some things from the past that are hindering you from moving forward and growing in your relationship with God?

6. How does forgiveness play a part in leaving the past behind? Is there anyone in your life you need to forgive?

Read **Hebrews 12:1-2** as a group:

Therefore we also, since we are surrounded by so great a cloud of witnesses, let us lay aside every weight, and the sin which so easily ensnares us, and let us run with endurance the race that is set before us, looking unto Jesus, the author and finisher of our faith, who for the joy that was set before Him endured the cross, despising the shame, and has sat down at the right hand of the throne of God.

7. Are there specific weights or sins in your life that easily ensnare you as you run your race? How can you lay them aside?

8. These verses emphasize "looking unto Jesus." When faced with life's distractions or discouragements, how can you redirect your focus onto Christ?

9. How does it resonate with you that Jesus is described as the "author and finisher of our faith?" In what ways does His example provide direction and encouragement in running your race with endurance?

10. We learned in this session that in order to run with intentionality and fulfill our God-given purpose, we must: 1. Run with a goal, 2. Run with a plan, and 3. Run with people. What is your goal, what is your plan, and who are your people?

GO TO GOD

Just as Paul turned to God for strength and clarity, let's also seek Him in our journey of intentional living. God, our Master Watchmaker, knows our purpose and desires for us to discover it.

Consider the following as you spend time with Him this week:

1. What weights from your past do you need to lay down in order to seek freedom and healing?

2. What is God's unique purpose for your life?

3. Pray for someone else, asking for God to help them in their challenges and trials.

4. Express gratitude for the race set before you, trusting that He who began a good work in you will complete it.

GET INTO ACTION

What are three tools or truths you took away from this session?

1. _____

2. _____

3. _____

What is the main thing you believe God wants you to apply?

_____

_____

_____

_____

_____

_____

_____

_____

_____

_____

_____

PRAYER AND PRAISE

Give each person a chance to share prayer requests and praise reports. Write your personal prayer requests and take notes on how you can pray for each other.

_____

_____

_____

_____

_____

_____

_____

_____

_____

_____

_____

_____

_____

_____

_____

_____

SESSION 4

DEVOTIONAL PLAN

DAY 22:
NO ROOM FOR DISPOSABLE CAMERAS

> *But what things were gain to me, these*
> *I have counted loss for Christ.*
> **PHILIPPIANS 3:7**

Do you remember disposable cameras? You would buy them before a vacation or special occasion, snap the pictures, and then have them developed in an hour. That certainly brings some nostalgia! One of the most popular brands was Kodak, but did you know they actually invented the first digital camera in 1975?

Today, from our phones to professional equipment, digital cameras are the primary game in town. So why did Kodak go bankrupt in 2012 after being the leader of an entire industry for over 100 years?

They focused on the wrong thing!

Rather than embrace their golden opportunity, they sacrificed their future by clinging to the status quo. Over time, they became irrelevant and were forced to shut their doors for good. Yes, focus matters in business. But Kodak's story reaches beyond the boardroom and into our homes, families, and spiritual lives as well.

The Apostle Paul could have easily lost focus in his life. He faced intense trials that could have derailed him and zapped his confidence and drive. He could've also been stuck in the shame and guilt of his past. But that's not what we see. Instead, we watch a man harness the power of focus, never losing sight of God's call. In turn, we can follow a life of intentionality and accomplishment.

Consider Paul's words in today's verse. He was saying that all of the trappings of status and success he used to cling to listed in verses 2-6 weren't really "gain" at all. Instead, they were "loss" when he compared his life to Jesus' mission for him.

When Paul met Jesus, he underwent a tectonic shift in what his life was really about. It transformed everything from the inside out. He ditched the "disposable camera" of his past pursuits to focus on the greatest prize and opportunity in the universe—following Jesus with everything he had!

REFLECT

I press toward the goal for the prize of the upward call of God in Christ Jesus. **Philippians 3:14**

To aid in your memorization, write out this week's memory verse:

_____

_____

Think about the people you look up to most in life. Are they driven by focus or derailed by distractions?

_____

_____

_____

_____

Does focus or distraction drive your daily life most? How so?

_____

_____

_____

_____

What is one area of distraction you can bring to Jesus to find eternal focus and perspective? What will that look like?

_____

_____

_____

_____

DAY 23:
FINDING FOCUS IN CHRIST

> *"...for he is a chosen vessel of Mine to bear My name before Gentiles, kings, and the children of Israel."*
> ACTS 9:15B

Do you feel like you're climbing a ladder, only to realize it's leaning against the wrong wall? Paul had an impressive resume and was zealous in his religious pursuits, but he was climbing the wrong ladder. Then came the Damascus Road encounter. Struck blind for three days, he received a new God-given mission. Scales fell from his eyes, both physically and spiritually. Jesus became the center of his life, redirecting his passions and pursuits for divine purposes.

Paul had to let go of his accolades and identity among peers to find his focus on Christ. Similarly, we may achieve worldly success but still lack spiritual significance. Like Paul, we have to submit our lives to the lordship of Christ to lead a determined and focused life.

Our relationship with Jesus is not a "cosmic killjoy." He is our ultimate coach. He gives us the power, perspective, and purpose we need to make an eternal impact. Just as a rudder guides a sailboat, let Christ be the rudder in your life, steering you in the right direction. We are His "chosen vessels."

The key to a fulfilling life isn't climbing the ladder of success, but instead making sure that ladder is propped against the right wall. In Christ, we find our true focus, where our passions and pursuits align with an eternal purpose.

REFLECT

Memory Verse

I press toward the goal for the prize of the upward call of God in Christ Jesus. **Philippians 3:14**

To aid in your memorization, write out this week's memory verse:

_____

_____

Do you feel like your ladder is leaning against the right or wrong wall? Why?

_____

_____

What are you holding on to that may be standing in the way of a focused life in Christ?

_____

_____

Is Christ the rudder in your life, or are you steering in your own direction?

_____

How is your relationship with Jesus affecting your daily decisions and long-term goals? Are there any changes you want to make in your relationship with God, decisions, and/or goals?

_____

_____

DAY 24:
GOODBYE TO CONDEMNATION

There is therefore now no condemnation to those who are in Christ Jesus...

ROMANS 8:1

Do your past failures and shortcomings haunt you, pulling down the sails of your confidence? Paul, a persecutor-turned-apostle, knew the weight of a past riddled with sin. So when he came back to the people he had once tormented, the air was thick with tension. Thoughts of unworthiness and guilt likely bombarded him. Yet, Paul encountered a life-changing truth—in Christ, our past loses its power over us!

Paul shares that message of total forgiveness in today's guiding verse. Imagine the freedom Paul felt knowing his past was redeemed and his conscience purified!

Much like Paul, we all have past failures that loom large in our minds. But the transformative power of Christ's forgiveness enables us to forgive ourselves and move forward. Don't drag around the burden of your past; Christ already carried it on the cross. Release it, and embrace the new life Jesus offers.

Your past may be filled with imperfect choices, but in Christ, you find forgiveness and freedom. Don't let your past be the anchor that drags you down; let Christ's forgiveness be the wind that fills your sails.

REFLECT

Memory Verse

I press toward the goal for the prize of the upward call of God in Christ Jesus. **Philippians 3:14**

To aid in your memorization, write out this week's memory verse:

_____

_____

How often do thoughts of your past interfere with your walk with Christ?

_____

_____

What do you need to release and forgive in yourself to fully embrace God's forgiveness?

_____

_____

Are you letting your past serve as a stumbling block or a stepping stone in your relationship with Christ?

_____

_____

How can you apply Paul's wisdom to 'forget what was behind' in your own life?

_____

_____

DAY 25:
ACCEPTING FORGIVENESS

Let us draw near with a true heart in full assurance of faith, having our hearts sprinkled from an evil conscience and our bodies washed with pure water.
HEBREWS 10:22

Yesterday we learned about our total freedom in Christ. However, even with that knowledge, that doesn't always stop our past from acting like a rearview mirror, distracting us from the road ahead.

Like Paul, we all have experiences or failures that can tether us to the past if we allow them. Forgiving ourselves and others is crucial; it frees us to focus on the present and future God has planned for us. Today's guiding verse reminds us that we can draw near to God with a clean conscience, as Jesus has washed us clean.

Imagine it like this—on a hot summer day, you were working on landscaping. Once finished, you come inside sweaty, muddy, and ready for a shower. What changes once you leave the water? You're clean, of course! You don't see dirt and mud caked on your arms in your reflection. Instead, your body has been washed. This is the picture of our lives in Christ.

Learning full forgiveness was a process for me. I forgave others and accepted God's forgiveness, but I struggled to forgive myself. Realizing that my future was clouded by this inability was a wake-up call. Letting go of my past was intricately tied to forgiving myself.

Don't let your past dictate your future. Choose to forgive, choose to release, and choose to press forward. Doing so will free you from the hindrance of past regrets, strengthen your faith, and prepare you for the journey ahead.

REFLECT

Memory Verse

I press toward the goal for the prize of the upward call of God in Christ Jesus. **Philippians 3:14**

To aid in your memorization, write out this week's memory verse:

_____

_____

Are you allowing past regrets to define your future?

_____

_____

_____

Have you truly forgiven yourself as Christ has forgiven you?

_____

_____

_____

Have you truly forgiven others? Who is someone you need to forgive?

_____

_____

_____

What steps can you take today to release your past and focus on what God has in store for you?

_____

_____

_____

How might your life change if you stopped looking in the rearview mirror and started focusing on the road ahead?

_____

_____

_____

I press toward the goal for the prize of the upward call of God in Christ Jesus.

Philippians 3:14

DAY 26:
THREE FEET FROM GOLD

> *Therefore do not cast away your confidence, which has great reward. For you have need of endurance, so that after you have done the will of God, you may receive the promise.*
> HEBREWS 10:35-36

Have you ever felt so weighed down by discouragement when you almost convinced yourself to just give up? I know it's hard to believe, but it's in these moments you might be closer to your breakthrough than you think.

Consider Darby, a man caught in the gold fever of the gold-rush days. After endless hours of digging, he found a promising vein of gold. Elated, he covered it up, raised funds for machinery, and began mining. But just when it seemed like he'd struck it rich, the vein disappeared. In the blink of an eye, everything he'd worked for vanished.

Desperate and disheartened, Darby and his team sold the machinery for scrap and went home defeated. But here's the twist—the man who bought the machinery consulted an engineer and found that Darby had stopped drilling just three feet from a massive vein of gold!

Today's guiding verse encourages us not to cast away our confidence but to endure. Unfathomably great rewards lie ahead. You might be facing challenges in your marriage, your career, or your walk with Christ. And just like Darby, you might be three feet from striking gold. The message is simple—if God's leading you, don't quit!

Don't be a Darby, giving up when you're just three feet from your "gold." Press on with confidence, enduring for the promises that God has for you.

REFLECT

I press toward the goal for the prize of the upward call of God in Christ Jesus. **Philippians 3:14**

To aid in your memorization, write out this week's memory verse:

_____

_____

Is there an area in your life where you feel like giving up? Could you be "three feet from gold"?

_____

_____

How might you refocus your efforts to endure and see it through?

_____

_____

Are your goals aligned with God's will for your life?

_____

_____

What would it take for you to place your confidence in God's promises and press on?

_____

_____

DAY 27:
A LIFESTYLE OF PERFECT PEACE

> *"You will keep him in perfect peace, whose mind is stayed on You, Because he trusts in You."*
> ISAIAH 26:3

Life has a way of snatching our peace, doesn't it? You're not alone if you've felt a knot in your stomach from yet another negative news story, or from racing thoughts when your head hits the pillow at night. The world doesn't pause to let us catch our breath; it moves with or without us, often stealing our peace in the process.

But today's guiding verse has a promise for you today! You can daily live in perfect peace. But how do we latch onto this peace? How can we embrace it and make it our own? We keep our minds "stayed" on Him. That's it. We never allow worry to steal our worship or allow problems to loom larger than the Prince of Peace.

Why do we have this peace? Because you are His child. You belong to the God who led Moses and the children of Israel through the Red Sea. The God who sent help to Daniel in the lion's den. Whatever the situation, God has helped millions of others find peace in similar circumstances.

Perfect peace is a lifestyle. And it's simpler to put into practice than you might think. Keep your mind "stayed" on God.

Morning Prayer
Before you even get out of bed, invite Jesus into your day. Ask Him to guide your thoughts, your actions, your words. If you're unsure where to start, keep it simple: "Father, please direct my day. Set my mind on Your presence above everything else!"

Mindful Moments
During the day, when stress tightens your chest, mentally step back and envision Jesus standing right beside you. What would He say?

The tough stuff of life might not immediately change. But your perspective will—and the starting point is knowing and declaring the promise that Jesus keeps in perfect peace, those whose mind is stayed on Him.

REFLECT

Memory Verse

I press toward the goal for the prize of the upward call of God in Christ Jesus. **Philippians 3:14**

To aid in your memorization, write out this week's memory verse:

_____

_____

When was the last time you felt true peace? What circumstances led to that moment?

_____

_____

What are some practical ways you can shift your focus from your worries to Jesus?

_____

_____

How can you integrate these steps into your daily routine to maintain a sense of peace?

_____

_____

What promises from God's Word can you hold onto during times of uncertainty and fear? Write down a few verses from the Bible.

_____

_____

WEEKLY REFLECTION

What are the top three realizations you had this session?

_____

_____

_____

_____

_____

_____

_____

What is the main thing you believe God wants you to apply?

_____

_____

_____

_____

_____

_____

_____

SESSION FIVE

What's happening outside cannot steal what God is doing inside.

SESSION 5 A Peaceful Life

In our culture of fear and worry, wouldn't it be nice to experience peace? This week, that is exactly what you can receive. A right-now peace. Peace beyond your understanding. Peace that doesn't come from our circumstances, but Christ Himself.

By diving into the wisdom of Isaiah and Paul, you'll discover that this profound peace isn't just a fleeting emotion—it's a steadfast promise from God. Together, we'll learn about the strength in praise, the comfort of prayer, and the impact of positive thinking. You'll see that so many worries stem from our limited perspective, not reality!

The key to it all? Trust. Trust in the One who gives a peace unlike any other. Let's take this journey hand in hand, stepping into a peace that's truly beyond words.

Weekend Message Notes And Questions

Use the following space to reflect on what you learned from the weekend message. Write down any questions you want to discuss with your small group.

_____

_____

_____

_____

_____

_____

_____

_____

_____

_____

_____

_____

_____

Getting Started

Peace is more than just a moment of calm. It's a deep-rooted trust in God, even when life feels uncertain. As we dive into Week Five, let's kick things off by discussing these questions:

• Describe a time in your life when you were truly at peace.

• What worries or challenges make it hard for you to feel God's peace and trust in His promises?

Watch The Lesson

Next is a space for notes, questions, and thoughts you want to share or remember. After watching the video, have someone read the lesson's discussion questions, then you can discuss them as a group. Remember to share the responsibilities of leading and reading each week.

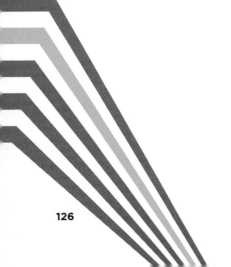

SESSION 5 Video Notes

Anxiety: To be distracted, divided, or pulled apart.

Matthew 6:25: *"Therefore I say to you, do not worry about your life, what you will eat or what you will drink; nor about your body, what you will put on. Is not life more than food and the body more than clothing?"*

Sources of Anxiety:

_____ Living

Legitimate _____

Irrational _____

How We Biblically Live Free Of Anxiety:

1. Bring your worries to God in _____.

Philippians 4:6: *Be anxious for nothing, but in everything by prayer and supplication, with thanksgiving, let your requests be made known to God.*

False **E**vidence **A**ppearing **R**eal.

2. Trade your worry for _____.

Philippians 4:6-7: *Be anxious for nothing, but in everything by prayer and supplication, with thanksgiving, let your requests be made known to God; and the peace of God, which surpasses all understanding, will guard your hearts and minds through Christ Jesus.*

3. Focus your mind on the _____.

Philippians 4:8: *Finally, brethren, whatever things are true, whatever things are noble, whatever things are just, whatever things are pure, whatever things are lovely, whatever things are of good report, if there is any virtue and if there is anything praiseworthy—meditate on these things.*

LET'S DISCUSS

In this section, discuss how you will apply the insights you've gained from the sermon and small group study. Then, talk about practical steps you can take to live out what you've learned.

Read **Isaiah 26:3** as a group:

> *"The steadfast of mind You will keep in perfect peace, because he trusts in You."*

1. What does it mean to have a "steadfast mind"?

Anxiety has become a significant challenge for many in our world today. What are some ways we can give our anxieties to God and receive His peace?

2. How does trust in God lead to perfect peace?

3. In what areas of your life do you struggle to trust God?

4. How can we trade our worry for worship?

Read **Philippians 4:8-9** as a group:

Finally, brethren, whatever is true, whatever is honorable, whatever is right, whatever is pure, whatever is lovely, whatever is of good repute, if there is any excellence and if anything worthy of praise, dwell on these things. The things you have learned and received and heard and seen in me, practice these things, and the God of peace will be with you.

5. How can focusing on these virtues impact our daily lives?

6. Why is it important to "dwell" on these things?

7. Can you share a time when pure and positive thinking changed your perspective?

8. How can we practice these principles in our daily interactions with others?

GO TO GOD

When we feel worried or scared, God's peace is a safe haven for our hearts and minds. He promises a special kind of peace that's deep and real. One that doesn't have its origin on earth. Best, He's there for our big worries and our everyday ones, too. Nothing is too big or too small to matter to God, or to see Him move.

Take time to:

1. Share where you're looking for peace in your life—maybe it's something that's been on your mind a lot.

2. Pray for your friends and family, and make a note to keep them in your prayers this week.

3. Talk about the good things happening in your life! What are you thankful for? How has God shown up for you?

GET INTO ACTION

What are three tools or truths you took away from this session?

1. _____

2. _____

3. _____

What is the main thing you believe God wants you to apply?

_____

_____

_____

_____

_____

_____

_____

_____

_____

_____

_____

PRAYER AND PRAISE

Give each person a chance to share prayer requests and praise reports. Write your personal prayer requests and take notes on how you can pray for each other.

_____

_____

_____

_____

_____

_____

_____

_____

_____

_____

_____

_____

_____

_____

SESSION 5

DEVOTIONAL PLAN

DAY 29:
THE SOUNDTRACK THAT BREAKS CHAINS

> *But at midnight Paul and Silas were praying and singing hymns to God, and the prisoners were listening to them. Suddenly there was a great earthquake, so that the foundations of the prison were shaken; and immediately all the doors were opened and everyone's chains were loosed.*
>
> ACTS 16:25-26

To the people in charge, Paul was a troublemaker. He was arrested multiple times, chased out of towns by angry residents, and was even the subject of a riot! All of this was in response to Paul's goal in life—sharing the Gospel.

In today's Scripture, we again find Paul in prison—this time with Silas. They had been dragged before Roman magistrates, falsely accused, beaten by an angry mob, had their clothes torn, and then thrown in jail.

Imagine yourself in their place for a moment. What would you be thinking about? What would you be talking about? How angry or afraid would you be? Remarkably, in the middle of the night, they were singing praises to God! Paul and Silas had every reason to despair. Yet, they understood that praise isn't just an emotional response, it's an act of the will.

Praise and worship shifts your focus off your problems onto God and His promises. Praise it isn't just for Sunday morning; it's the soundtrack that should fill our lives. Unlike silent forms of worship, praise is vocal and expressive.

Consider it like this. If your child achieved something great, you wouldn't quietly applaud. You'd celebrate loudly, sharing the good news with anyone willing to listen. The same goes for praising God.

Today, take a moment to vocalize your praise. Whether it's through a spoken prayer or a song, let it be heard. List three things you're grateful for and intentionally praise God for them. Then watch how this small act shifts both your perspective and the atmosphere around you.

REFLECT

Memory Verse

Be anxious for nothing, but in everything by prayer and supplication, with thanksgiving, let your requests be made known to God; and the peace of God, which surpasses all understanding, will guard your hearts and minds through Christ Jesus. **Philippians 4:6-7**

To aid in your memorization, write out this week's memory verse:

_____

_____

_____

_____

What situations in your life are weighing you down and how can praising God change your perspective?

_____

_____

_____

_____

How can you make praising God a consistent part of your daily life?

_____

_____

_____

_____

What are some ways you can vocalize your praise, rather than keeping it inward?

_____

_____

_____

_____

Are there specific blessings you've overlooked that deserve your vocal praise?

_____

_____

_____

_____

DAY 30:
THREE TYPES OF PRAYER

Be anxious for nothing, but in everything by prayer and supplication, with thanksgiving, let your requests be made known to God; and the peace of God, which surpasses all understanding, will guard your hearts and minds through Christ Jesus.

PHILIPPIANS 4:6-7

Anxiety has a way of chaining our hearts and minds, doesn't it? Imagine if you had the key to unlock those chains. According to Paul, that key is in three types of prayer—devotion, supplication, and intercession.

The act of prayer is more than just a wish list to God; it's an intimate conversation that releases you from the grip of anxiety. It's not just you talking to God, but also pausing to listen to Him. Prayer is a transfer station where we unload our worries and receive God's peace in return.

Scripture introduces us to various types of prayer—devotion, supplication, and intercession. In devotional prayer, you commune with God, basking in His love. Through supplication, you present your needs before God, trusting Him to provide. Intercession is where you stand in the gap for others, lifting their needs to God.

One significant step towards peace is understanding 'supplication.' Here, you are not just wishing away problems; you're actively releasing them to God. The moment we do this, an incredible emotional and mental weight lifts, replaced by a peace that transcends understanding.

Today, engage in a three-part prayer cycle—start with a devotional prayer to connect with God. Proceed to supplication, where you list your concerns and surrender them to Him. Lastly, practice intercession by praying for someone else's needs. Note the sense of peace that envelops you afterward.

REFLECT

Be anxious for nothing, but in everything by prayer and supplication, with thanksgiving, let your requests be made known to God; and the peace of God, which surpasses all understanding, will guard your hearts and minds through Christ Jesus. **Philippians 4:6-7**

To aid in your memorization, write out this week's memory verse:

_____

_____

_____

_____

What specific anxieties have you been holding onto that need to be released in prayer?

_____

_____

How often do you pause to listen to God during your prayer time?

_____

How can you incorporate various types of prayer like devotion, supplication, and intercession in your daily time with God?

_____

Who can you intercede for today, and what are their specific needs?

_____

DAY 31:
OVERCOME THE ANXIETY CYCLE

> *Casting all your anxiety on Him,*
> *because He cares for you.*
> **1 PETER 5:7 (NIV)**

Researchers define anxiety as "apprehension, tension, or uneasiness that stems from the anticipation of danger." So when we're anxious, we're scared. Anxiousness produces fear. From there, it propels through an unending cycle:

1. Anxiety influences our thought life.

2. Our thought life creates our emotional state.

3. Our emotional state influences our words and actions.

4. Our words and actions create our outcomes.

5. Our outcomes define the quality of our lives–peace or anxiety. *Then repeat!*

Do you see how anxiety shapes your life? The good news is, God doesn't merely point out this problem—He tells us what to do about it.

The Greek term for "anxiety" – merimna – implies a "divided mind." Imagine your mind as a pie divided into slices of distractions, worries, fears, and burdens. The result is not just a lack of focus, but a loss of "traction" towards your God-given purpose. Think of distraction as "dis-traction"—losing grip and traction on your destiny.

This is where God steps in. He invites us to cast, or throw forcefully, our anxieties onto Him. By doing so, we can experience an inner harmony that aligns our divided mind. What results is an integrated mind, undivided and focused, no longer distracted by anxieties but empowered by God's peace. When peace and focus partner together, they create an effective antidote to anxiety and distraction.

Today, set aside ten minutes to sit quietly and list down all the things causing you anxiety. Now, physically cross them off and mentally cast them upon God in prayer. Declare His peace over your life and make a conscious choice to remain focused on your purpose.

REFLECT

Be anxious for nothing, but in everything by prayer and supplication, with thanksgiving, let your requests be made known to God; and the peace of God, which surpasses all understanding, will guard your hearts and minds through Christ Jesus. **Philippians 4:6-7**

To aid in your memorization, write out this week's memory verse:

_____

_____

_____

_____

Which common anxieties are currently fragmenting your mind and focus?

_____

_____

_____

_____

How have these anxieties disrupted your pursuit of your God-given purpose?

_____

_____

_____

_____

What practical steps can you take to remain focused amid life's distractions?

_____

_____

_____

_____

After casting your anxieties on God, what changes do you observe in your level of peace and focus?

_____

_____

_____

_____

DAY 32:
A POWERFUL POSITIVITY "CHECKLIST"

> *Finally, brethren, whatever is true, whatever is honorable, whatever is right, whatever is pure, whatever is lovely, whatever is of good repute, if there is any excellence and if anything worthy of praise, dwell on these things.*
> PHILIPPIANS 4:8 (NASB)

Positivity helps our spiritual hearts. Did you know it also helps our physical hearts?

A Johns Hopkins study found that positive thinking reduces the risk of a heart attack by 33 percent in people with a family history of heart disease! Our mindset truly changes everything. Which is exactly what today's guiding verse helps us do. Paul provides us attributes of godly thinking we can use as a quick "checklist" to guide our thought life:

True: *Does this align with God's Word?*
Psalm 19:7; John 16:13; 2 Timothy 3:16–17

Honorable: *Does this bring respect to yourself and others?*
Proverbs 22:1; Romans 12:10; 1 Peter 2:12

Right: *Is it just and fair?*
Micah 6:8; Romans 12:2; Proverbs 21:3

Pure: *Is it free from moral fault?*
Psalm 51:10; Philippians 4:8; James 3:17

Lovely: *Does it promote love and compassion?*
1 Corinthians 16:14; Colossians 3:12–14; 1 John 4:7

Praiseworthy: *Is it deserving of admiration and respect?*
Psalm 145:3; Ephesians 1:12; Philippians 2:3

To Paul, who is writing to the Philippians from jail, these aren't abstract ideals; they are the practical means of a peace-filled life! So, my friend, what thoughts are guiding your life?

I encourage you to write these attributes down, print them out, jot them in a note on your phone, put them on sticky notes to place on your computer! Take a simple step to keep them in front of you. "Dwell on these things" daily as an exercise to begin shifting your thought life (and even help your heart in the process).

REFLECT

Be anxious for nothing, but in everything by prayer and supplication, with thanksgiving, let your requests be made known to God; and the peace of God, which surpasses all understanding, will guard your hearts and minds through Christ Jesus. **Philippians 4:6-7**

To aid in your memorization, write out this week's memory verse:

_____

_____

_____

_____

What are the predominant thoughts that guide your life?

_____

_____

_____

_____

How might you practically incorporate Paul's checklist into your day?

_____

_____

_____

_____

Is there a particular area from the checklist where you feel you're lacking?

_____

_____

_____

_____

What Scripture can you memorize to help anchor your thoughts?

_____

_____

_____

_____

DAY 33:
PRESS YOUR WORRY-REMOVAL BUTTON

> *Search me, O God, and know my heart;*
> *Try me and know my anxieties;*
> **PSALM 139:23**

What if you could press a button and remove over 90 percent of your anxiety? How often would you press it? I'll be honest, some days, mine would be worn out!

Statistics suggest that 92 percent of stress and fear is based on our mental perceptions—things that will likely never happen or can't be changed. Here's the breakdown:

Future events that will probably never happen | 40 percent
Past events that can't be changed | 30 percent
Criticism from others, mostly untrue | 12 percent
State of our health, which worsens with stress | 10 percent
Real problems we must face | 8 percent

We spend so much energy *worrying* when we could be *trusting* God, Who knows and provides for all our needs. So, here are your worry-removal buttons to press:

Self-Awareness: Psalm 139:23 urges us to ask God to reveal our anxious thoughts. A moment of prayer can illuminate your underlying worries, most of which are irrational.

Fill your mind with Truth: God's Word is full of truths that can replace these anxieties. The Bible offers peace that transcends understanding, guidance on how to live, and wisdom on what truly matters.

Try this whenever you feel anxious, panicked, or stressed this week—pause, press, and trust God to bless the rest!

REFLECT

Memory Verse

Be anxious for nothing, but in everything by prayer and supplication, with thanksgiving, let your requests be made known to God; and the peace of God, which surpasses all understanding, will guard your hearts and minds through Christ Jesus. **Philippians 4:6-7**

To aid in your memorization, write out this week's memory verse:

_____

_____

_____

_____

What are the most common worries that occupy your mind?

_____

_____

How often do you turn to God when you feel anxious?

_____

_____

What thoughts can you "pause and press" right now?

_____

_____

_____

DAY 34:
GOD'S COVENANT OF PEACE

> *"..For the mountains shall depart and the hills be removed, but My kindness shall not depart from you, nor shall My covenant of peace be removed,"* says the LORD, who has mercy on you.
>
> ISAIAH 54:10

Imagine a world where Mount Rushmore vanishes into thin air. Sounds impossible, right? Yet, God assures us that there's a higher chance of that happening than losing His kindness and peace!

In a world built upon quicksand, God's promise stands firm: He offers us an unbreakable covenant of peace. This is so important to Him, His peace is mentioned over 350 times in Scripture!

The word *peace* is our best translation of the Hebrew word *shalom*. It means "nothing broken, nothing missing." It's complete and perfect peace, safety, prosperity, wellness, and health.

Shalom assures us that in God's Kingdom there's provision for lack or brokenness. So when you're grappling with financial worries, family conflicts, or business challenges, remember that God's covenant of peace is with you. Even when the world around us is in chaos, His peace remains steadfast. What's happening outside does not have to steal what God is doing inside.

In John 14:27, Jesus informed the disciples He would be crucified. To them, it felt like a final defeat. But Jesus offered a perspective shift: *"Peace I leave with you; My peace I give to you; not as the world gives do I give to you. Do not let your heart be troubled, nor let it be fearful."*

This peace is the cornerstone of the abundant life Jesus promises (John 10:10). No matter how big the "mountains" are that fall around us, God's peace is sure as tomorrow's sunrise.

REFLECT

Be anxious for nothing, but in everything by prayer and supplication, with thanksgiving, let your requests be made known to God; and the peace of God, which surpasses all understanding, will guard your hearts and minds through Christ Jesus. **Philippians 4:6-7**

To aid in your memorization, write out this week's memory verse:

_____

_____

_____

_____

In what areas of your life do you need to invite God's covenant of peace today?

_____

_____

How can you actively remind yourself of God's promise of "shalom" in challenging times?

_____

_____

Will you commit to reading or memorizing Jesus' promise in John 14:27 this week?

_____

_____

WEEKLY REFLECTION

What are the top three realizations you had this session?

_____

_____

_____

_____

_____

_____

What is the main thing you believe God wants you to apply?

_____

_____

_____

_____

_____

_____

SESSION SIX

If we cannot be content and embrace where we are today, we will never be ready to move into our tomorrows.

SESSION 6 A Content Life

In a world that constantly pushes for more, have you ever wondered what it means to be truly satisfied?

This week, we're diving into the heart of contentment. It's about a perspective shift, seeing our lives through a lens of gratitude for what we have, rather than an absence of something we want.

Together, we'll uncover the subtle enemies of contentment, like unchecked worries and the trap of comparison. Paul's letter to the Philippians will help us understand that contentment isn't about having everything, but experiencing joy in the midst of any situation.

Because our real work isn't just getting more; it's embracing the joy that comes from trusting in God's plan and gratitude for what we have.

Weekend Message Notes And Questions

Use the following space to reflect on what you learned from the weekend message. Write down any questions you want to discuss with your small group.

_____

_____

_____

_____

_____

_____

_____

_____

_____

_____

_____

_____

_____

_____

SMALL GROUP A Content Life

Getting Started

In our culture's pursuit of more, it can be easy to lose sight of the blessings right in front of us. As we dive into this week's topic on contentment, let's begin by reflecting on our own lives:

• What are some things you're truly grateful for right now?

• Can you recall a time when you felt content even when you didn't have everything you wanted?

Watch The Lesson

Next is a space for notes, questions, and thoughts you want to share or remember. After watching the video, have someone read the lesson's discussion questions, then you can discuss them as a group. Remember to share the responsibilities of leading and reading each week.

Enemies of Contentment:

1. _____

Mark 4:19: *"And the cares of this world, the deceitfulness of riches, and the desires for other things entering in choke the word, and it becomes unfruitful."*

2. _____

2 Corinthians 10:12 (NIV): *We do not dare to classify or compare ourselves with some who commend themselves. When they measure themselves by themselves and compare themselves with themselves, they are not wise.*

Philippians 4:10-13: *But I rejoiced in the Lord greatly that now at last your care for me has flourished again; though you surely did care, but you lacked opportunity. [11] Not that I speak in regard to need, for I have learned in whatever state I am, to be content: [12] I know how to be abased, and I know how to abound. Everywhere and in all things I have learned both to be full and to be hungry, both to abound and to suffer need. [13] I can do all things through Christ who strengthens me.*

Three Secrets to Contentment:

1. Contentment is _____.

Philippians 4:11: *Not that I speak in regard to need, for I have learned in whatever state I am, to be content.*

2. Contentment stems from _____.

Philippians 4:12: *I know how to be abased, and I know how to abound. Everywhere and in all things I have learned both to be full and to be hungry, both to abound and to suffer need.*

1 Thessalonians 5:18: *In everything give thanks; for this is the will of God in Christ Jesus for you.*

3. Contentment comes as we _____

Philippians 4:13: *I can do all things through Christ who strengthens me*

LET'S DISCUSS

Read these verses as a group. Then, dive deeper into this week's focus on contentment by discussing the questions and sharing how you can apply these truths.

Read **Philippians 4:10–13** as a group:

But I rejoiced in the Lord greatly that now at last your care for me has flourished again; though you surely did care, but you lacked opportunity. Not that I speak in regard to need, for I have learned in whatever state I am, to be content: I know how to be abased, and I know how to abound. Everywhere and in all things I have learned both to be full and to be hungry, both to abound and to suffer need. I can do all things through Christ who strengthens me.

1. What stands out to you about Paul's perspective on contentment?

2. How does Paul's situation and response challenge our modern views on happiness and satisfaction?

3. Can you recall any past circumstances or situations where finding contentment was a challenge for you? Share.

4. In what ways can we apply Paul's mindset to our own lives, especially when facing challenges?

5. How does relying on Christ's strength relate to finding contentment?

Read **1 Thessalonians 5:18** as a group:

In everything give thanks; for this is the will of God in Christ Jesus for you.

6. Why do you think gratitude is highlighted as God's will for us?

7. How can practicing gratitude daily change our perspective and feelings of contentment?

8. Can you share a personal experience where gratitude shifted your mindset during a challenging time?

9. How can we support each other in cultivating a habit of thankfulness in our daily lives?

GO TO GOD

No matter our starting place, connecting with God brings us back to a place of peace and contentment. He's always there, ready for us to reach out, to lay down our worries, and to find joy in His presence.

Take time to:

1. Reflect on areas in your life where you've felt discontent. Offer these up in prayer, asking God to help you find contentment in Him.

2. Think of someone you know who's struggling with contentment. Pray for them, asking God to provide them with peace and a fresh perspective.

3. Celebrate the moments of joy and contentment you've experienced recently. Thank God for these blessings and ask Him to help you recognize more of them in your daily life.

4. Ask God to help you trust in His plan, even when things don't go as expected. Remember, He has a purpose for every season of our lives.

GET INTO ACTION

What are three tools or truths you took away from this session?

1. _____

2. _____

3. _____

What is the main thing you believe God wants you to apply?

_____

_____

_____

_____

_____

_____

_____

_____

_____

_____

_____

PRAYER AND PRAISE

Give each person a chance to share prayer requests and praise reports. Write your personal prayer requests and take notes on how you can pray for each other.

_____

_____

_____

_____

_____

_____

_____

_____

_____

_____

_____

_____

_____

_____

SESSION 6

DEVOTIONAL PLAN

DAY 36:
ENEMIES OF CONTENTMENT

> *Yet indeed I also count all things loss for the excellence of the knowledge of Christ Jesus my Lord, for whom I have suffered the loss of all things, and count them as rubbish, that I may gain Christ.*
> **PHILIPPIANS 3:8**

Does the phrase "If only…" often preface your wishes and desires?

If only I were younger…
If only I had a different job…
If only I had that special someone…
If only I had a bigger house…
If only I had gone to college…

The false promise of "if only" thinking is: "If I only had that thing, I'd be happy." It's a mindset many of us know all too well, one that blocks the way to true contentment. We can define contentment this way—to be independent of external circumstances, content with one's lot, with one's means. God tells us that's a really good thing (1 Timothy 6:6–10).

This truth resonated with Paul so deeply that it transformed how he saw everything. The if onlys of life became loss rather than gain. Rather than being driven by supreme willpower or stoic strength, Paul was drawn to the contentment we can all find in Christ.

In my life, I've noticed two significant enemies that constantly attack godly contentment:

Enemy #1: Cares of the World

Anxiety undermines trust in God's provision and wisdom. Jesus warns in Mark 4:19 that "cares of this world" can choke God's Word and promises in our lives, rendering them unfruitful.

Enemy #2: Comparison

This ever-present enemy is a thief of joy. As Paul notes in 2 Corinthians 10:12, comparing ourselves to others is unwise. There will always be someone with something "better," keeping us in a never-ending cycle of discontentment.

This week, whenever the thought "If only..." enters your mind, replace it with gratitude. Make a daily gratitude list or share with someone just one thing you are thankful for, no matter how small. An attitude of gratitude is a powerful weapon against the enemies of our contentment!

REFLECT

Memory Verse

Not that I speak in regard to need, for I have learned in whatever state I am, to be content. **Philippians 4:11**

To aid in your memorization, write out this week's memory verse:

_____

_____

What are the "If only..." statements you frequently catch yourself thinking?

_____

_____

_____

_____

Are your cares based on things within your control? How can you surrender them to God?

_____

_____

_____

_____

In what areas of your life do you most frequently find yourself making comparisons?

_____

_____

_____

_____

How can remembering God's provision in the past help you become more content in the present?

_____

_____

_____

_____

DAY 37:
LEARNING CONTENTMENT

> ***...for I have learned in whatever***
> ***state I am, to be content.***
> **PHILIPPIANS 4:11**

You don't need to enroll in an elite university to study one of life's most valuable subjects—contentment. Unlike built-in car features, contentment isn't something you "have or don't have." It's a lesson to be learned; one that Paul himself learned. I've found it helpful to break it down into four parts.

One: Contentment is a "Now" Thing

First, let's steer clear of equating contentment with "having" or "getting" enough things. Anything we put between us and godly contentment misses the point.

Two: Contentment is About Abundant Life

However, contentment isn't a blissful enlightenment where we disconnect from the world. Jesus doesn't lead us to a state of cosmic emptiness, but a life full of joy and peace beyond understanding. He puts it like this in John 10:10b: *"...I have come that they may have life, and that they may have it more abundantly."* He fills us up rather than emptying us out.

Three: Contentment Isn't Complacent

Contentment is not about being complacent; it's about savoring today to its fullest while stewarding what God has given us. Think of contentment as the art of enjoying every last drop of your hot fudge sundae. It's about maximum joy and satisfaction from what God has given you today and positioning you for tomorrow.

Four: Contentment Sets You Free

Contentment doesn't hold you back... it sets you free. When we learn to find our contentment in God, we're not sidelined; we're set up for promotion in God's Kingdom. You're ready for tomorrow when you learn to be content today. Being content today doesn't mean we cease to grow or aim for better; it means we do so without the chains of discontentment weighing us down.

REFLECT

Not that I speak in regard to need, for I have learned in whatever state I am, to be content. **Philippians 4:11**

To aid in your memorization, write out this week's memory verse:

_____

_____

What does the word "contentment" mean to you? How does your definition align or differ with Paul's teachings in Philippians 4:11?

_____

_____

_____

_____

What is currently the biggest obstacle to your contentment? Is it external circumstances or internal discontent?

_____

_____

_____

_____

Do you find yourself frequently comparing your life to others? How does this impact your sense of contentment or dissatisfaction?

_____

_____

_____

_____

DAY 38:
RADICAL GRATITUDE

I know how to be abased, and I know how to abound. Everywhere and in all things, I have learned both to be full and to be hungry, both to abound and to suffer need.
PHILIPPIANS 4:12

Imagine two children at Christmas. One eagerly rips open a present and exclaims, "Thank you, this is awesome!" The other mutters, "Is that all?"

Same celebration, two very different attitudes. The difference? Gratitude. The same holds true away from the Christmas tree. Ever noticed how some people seem to glow with an inner peace, regardless of life's ups and downs? Like the Apostle Paul, they've discovered a secret, and it starts in the heart.

Paul didn't say life was easy. He said he "learned" how to be content in any circumstance. Gratitude is about perspective. Paul tells us that whether he was up or down, well-fed or hungry, he found a way to be grateful. As the saying goes, the heart of the matter is the matter of the heart.

Gratefulness is a choice, and it doesn't depend on the abundance or lack of material things. Things change. Things break. Things are fleeting. But a grateful heart? That's eternal.

Jesus described what this kind of life looks like in Matthew 6:19–21:

"Do not lay up for yourselves treasures on earth, where moth and rust destroy and where thieves break in and steal, but lay up for yourselves treasures in heaven, where neither moth nor rust destroys and where thieves do not break in and steal. For where your treasure is, there your heart will be also."

Biblical gratitude is radical when you understand that everything on Earth has an expiration date. The surest things, highest-quality possessions, and even good health won't last. But our heavenly riches cannot be taken away.

Like those two kids at Christmas, our lives reflect our hearts. Where is your treasure?

REFLECT

Not that I speak in regard to need, for I have learned in whatever state I am, to be content. **Philippians 4:11**

To aid in your memorization, write out this week's memory verse:

_____

_____

How does your level of contentment compare to the Apostle Paul's, who was content in any circumstance?

_____

_____

_____

_____

What is preventing you from having a grateful heart today?

_____

_____

_____

_____

How might clinging to material things obstruct your spiritual growth?

_____

_____

_____

What's one actionable step you can take today to cultivate a more grateful heart?

_____

_____

_____

_____

DAY 39:
THE DISCIPLINE OF GRATITUDE

> ### *In everything give thanks; for this is the will of God in Christ Jesus for you.*
> #### 1 THESSALONIANS 5:18

If you've ever found yourself pondering God's will for your life, the answer begins with a heart filled with gratitude.

Ever felt like your life was missing something? Like you're running on a treadmill, always seeking but never finding? It might surprise you, but the first step off of that treadmill starts with two simple words: "Thank you."

Paul meant it when he said, "In everything give thanks." We learned he had his share of hardships—imprisonments, beatings, and shipwrecks—just to name a few. Yet he knew that gratitude wasn't just a self-help tip for a better day, it was God's will.

So take a moment. Reflect on the blessings you overlook. Did you graduate from high school, college, or even grad school? Do you have a job you're passionate about? Is your health more of a blessing than a burden? Do you have a good friend? A spouse? A loving family?

If you're nodding to even a few of these, you're richer than you think. You're in the world's top ten percent! Let's not squander these gifts by dreaming about everything we don't have. Instead, let's cultivate a grateful heart. Gratitude is a discipline—a use-it-or-lose-it muscle we train every day. However, even if you feel like your gratitude muscle hasn't been worked out in a while, it's so simple to get back into action.

Starting with "Thank you" doesn't change what you have, it changes the way you see what you have. A grateful heart sees every day as a gift. Thankfulness trains your mind to shift your focus from your burdens to your blessings.

REFLECT

Not that I speak in regard to need, for I have learned in whatever state I am, to be content. **Philippians 4:11**

To aid in your memorization, write out this week's memory verse:

_____

_____

What are the top three things you're most grateful for right now?

_____

_____

When you feel discontent, how do you typically respond? Could integrating a moment of gratitude change your perspective?

_____

_____

Have you ever kept a gratitude journal? If so, how did it affect your daily life and emotional well-being?

_____

_____

How can you share the power of gratitude with others? Are there specific ways you can express thankfulness in your interactions?

_____

DAY 40:

> *I can do all things through Christ who strengthens me.*
> **PHILIPPIANS 4:13**

About 900 years ago, a boy named Francis was born into a tremendously wealthy family. He grew up with all the trappings of success, comfort, and affluence. Then, something profound happened—he met Jesus. This led him on a journey of leaving everything to pursue the greater things of God. You may be familiar with this boy, he grew up to be called St. Francis of Assisi.

While being a disciple of Jesus isn't about how much, or how little, money is in your bank account, it is about our affections. In Matthew 19:16–22, a rich and virtuous young man asked Jesus how to find eternal life. In verse 21, Jesus said, *"If you want to be perfect, go, sell what you have and give to the poor, and you will have treasure in heaven; and come, follow Me."* However, unlike Francis, the young man "went away sorrowful, for he had great possessions."

The truth is, the young ruler didn't own possessions as much as they owned him. Whether you look more like Francis or the young man, Paul shared the secret to *contentment* in today's verse—the strength of Christ working in us!

We often associate Philippians 4:13 with overcoming obstacles, but its biblical context is Paul's message of contentment. God gives us the strength to be content because we are wholly incapable of finding it ourselves. But true contentment in a culture of *more, more, more* is a hallmark of God's people!

Contentment makes us beacons of joy like cities set on a hill that can't be hidden. In either crisis or comfort, contentment is a powerful witness to God's strength working within you. It can be one of the most powerful ways you share your faith with the people in your life who desperately need the hope of Jesus!

REFLECT

Memory Verse

Not that I speak in regard to need, for I have learned in whatever state I am, to be content. **Philippians 4:11**

To aid in your memorization, write out this week's memory verse:

_____

_____

Which life is more appealing to you—Francis' or the young man's? Why?

_____

_____

_____

Do your possessions own you more than you own them? How does that show up in your life?

_____

_____

_____

Is there anything in your life God is calling you to leave behind so you can experience true contentment?

_____

_____

_____

DAY 41:
CURING DESTINATION DISEASE

Now godliness with contentment is great gain.
1 TIMOTHY 6:6

Have you ever heard the saying, "Wherever you are, be there"? It's about being present in every place and with every person. Instead of being troubled by the past or anxious about the future, you're fully engaged right where you are. Research shows that being fully present actually predicts greater positive emotional states in the long run. We sacrifice future wellbeing when we don't savor the present.

That's a powerful thought—especially for someone like me who has suffered from what I call "Destination Disease!" It's that feeling when you're walking along a beautiful beach on vacation and you wonder, "Where can we go to next?!"

The truth is, contentment doesn't depend on your zip code. A geographical cure is a mirage. Whether you're in the Rockies dreaming about ocean waves or on the beach envisioning snowy peaks, moving locations won't bring peace to your soul. It's an illusion, not a cure for the discontented spirit.

We often suffer from "Destination Disease," thinking life will be perfect once we arrive at a certain point—financially, relationally, or geographically. But contentment isn't about arriving; it's about thriving where you are. God strengthens us in the process, not just at the destination.

So, my friend, wherever you are today, be there!

REFLECT

Memory Verse

Not that I speak in regard to need, for I have learned in whatever state I am, to be content. **Philippians 4:11**

To aid in your memorization, write out this week's memory verse:

_____

_____

What are some "geographical cures" you've thought about or even tried? Did they work?

_____

_____

_____

Do you find yourself waiting for the next big thing to happen before you can be content? How can you break this cycle?

_____

_____

_____

How can you cultivate contentment in your current situation, instead of looking elsewhere for happiness?

_____

_____

_____

WEEKLY REFLECTION

What are the top three realizations you had this session?

_____

_____

_____

_____

_____

_____

What is the main thing you believe God wants you to apply?

_____

_____

_____

_____

_____

_____

APPENDICES

APPENDICES

Resources to make your small group experience excellent!

FREQUENTLY ASKED QUESTIONS

WHAT DO WE DO IN THE FIRST GROUP?

Make sure everyone in your group has the opportunity to introduce themselves and share what they are expecting from this study. But most importantly, have fun as your study begins.

WHERE DO I FIND NEW MEMBERS FOR THE GROUP?

This can be challenging, especially for new groups that only have a few people or for existing groups that lose a few people along the way. We encourage you to pray with your group and then brainstorm a list of people from work, church, your neighborhood, your children's school, family, the gym, and so forth. Have each group member invite several of the people on his or her list. No matter how you find members, it is vital to stay on the lookout for new people to join your group. All groups tend to go through healthy transitions—the results of moves, releasing new leaders, ministry opportunities, and situations and opportunities that arise. If you and your group stay open, you will be amazed at the people God sends your way.

WHO IS THE SMALL GROUP LEADER?

Each group has an official leader who facilitates the group. But ideally, the group will mature, and members will share the small group leader role. This model ensures all members grow, give their unique contribution, and develop their gifts. The small group discussion and the Holy Spirit can keep things on track even when you rotate leaders. Christ has promised to be in your midst as you gather.

CAN I DO THIS STUDY ON MY OWN?

You sure can, but you may choose to gather with co-workers, family members, or a few friends who would enjoy the connection. The Holy Spirit will be with you even if there are only two of you. (See Matthew 18:20)

WHAT IF THIS GROUP IS NOT WORKING FOR ME?

You are not alone! This could be the result of a personality conflict, life-stage difference, geographical distance, level of spiritual maturity, or any number of things. Relax. Pray for God's direction, and at the end of this six-week study, decide whether to continue with this group or find another. Also, do not run from conflict or pre-judge people before you have given them a chance. God is still working in your life, too!

HOW LONG WILL THIS GROUP MEET?

Groups meet every week throughout the six-week Perspective Shift series. At the end of this study, each group member may decide if he or she wants to continue on for another study. Some groups launch relationships for years to come, and others are stepping-stones into another small group. Either way, enjoy the journey.

HOW DO WE HANDLE THE CHILDCARE NEEDS IN OUR GROUP?

We suggest you empower the group to brainstorm solutions openly. You may try one option that works for a while and then adjust over time. A favorite approach is for adults to meet in the living room or dining room and to share the cost of a babysitter (or two) who can watch the kids in a different part of the house. This way, parents do not have to be away from their children all evening when their children are too young to be left at home. A second option is to use one home for the kids and a second home (close by or a phone call away) for the adults. Finally, the most common solution is to decide you need to have a night to invest in your spiritual lives and to make arrangements for childcare. No matter what decision the group makes, the best approach is to dialogue openly about both the problem and the solution.

SMALL GROUP GUIDELINES

It is a good idea to begin the small group with clear guidelines and expectations. These guidelines will help each person understand the group's goals and lay a foundation for a healthy group experience. Please take a few moments to review the guidelines the group is to agree upon.

COMMUNITY: Spiritually and relationally grow in the context of a small group community.

ATTENDANCE: Make a commitment to attend the group each week.

SAFE ENVIRONMENT: Create a safe, non-judgmental place for people to come and feel loved.

CONFIDENTIALITY: Keep everything shared in the group in the group.

INVITE OTHERS: Invite friends and new people to the group and warmly welcome newcomers.

USE WISDOM: Commit to using wisdom by not serving or consuming alcohol during small group meetings to avoid causing a brother or sister to stumble spiritually. Be sensitive to others' spiritual conscience. (See 1 Corinthians 8:1-13; Romans 14:19-21.)

SHARED OWNERSHIP: Remember, it's important for each attendee to share a small team role or responsibility over the course of the study.

A NOTE TO SMALL GROUP LEADERS:

You may want to provide name tags for at least the first meeting.

Open your group with a brief, simple prayer. Invite God to open your spiritual eyes and to give you insight as you study. You can pray for specific requests at the end of the meeting or stop momentarily to pray if a particular situation comes up during your discussion.

After the opening prayer, review the Small Group Guidelines in the Appendices with the entire group. To lay the foundation for a healthy small group experience, it's a good idea to begin the first session with clear guidelines and expectations.

Next, get contact information from every person in the group. You may pass around the Small Group Roster found in the Appendices, or use a sheet of paper. Ask someone in the group to make copies or type up the roster and email it to the group members during the week.

Plan to rotate who leads the group discussion after the first week. Studies have shown that healthy groups share the load. This helps to develop every member's ability to lead a few people in a safe environment. Jesus consistently gave others the opportunity to serve alongside Him. (See Mark 6:30-44.)

Study the rest of the Appendices for additional information about leading the group.

PRAYER OF SALVATION

The following prayer is an example of a prayer of salvation. If you or someone you know has decided to follow Christ, use this prayer as a guide to accepting God's forgiveness and committing to follow Him.

Dear Jesus, I come to You today, a sinner, in need of a Savior. Thank You, Jesus, for dying on the cross for me, for shedding Your blood for me. Jesus, I let go of my past, I turn to You, I turn to the cross. Come into my life. Forgive me. Wash me. Cleanse me with Your blood. Jesus, I take my life, and I put it into Your hands. From this day forward, I belong to You. Amen.

MEMORY VERSES

Commit these verses to memory and see the Word of God come alive in you!

SESSION ONE

...Let this mind be in you which was also in Christ Jesus.
Philippians 2:5

SESSION TWO

For to me, to live is Christ, and to die is gain.
Philippians 1:21

SESSION THREE

Let nothing be done through selfish ambition or conceit, but in lowliness of mind let each esteem others better than himself. Let each of you look out not only for his own interests, but also for the interests of others.
Philippians 2:3-4

SESSION FOUR

I press toward the goal for the prize of the upward call of God in Christ Jesus. **Philippians 3:14**

SESSION FIVE

Be anxious for nothing, but in everything by prayer and supplication, with thanksgiving, let your requests be made known to God; and the peace of God, which surpasses all understanding, will guard your hearts and minds through Christ Jesus. **Philippians 4:6-7**

SESSION SIX

Not that I speak in regard to need, for I have learned in whatever state I am, to be content. **Philippians 4:11**

SMALL GROUP LEADER TIPS

Congratulations! You have responded to the call to lead a *Perspective Shift* group. As you prepare to lead, here are a few thoughts to keep in mind:

REMEMBER, YOU ARE NOT ALONE.

God knows everything about you, and He knew you would be asked to lead your group. Remember, it is common for all good leaders to feel they are not ready. Moses, Solomon, Jeremiah, and Timothy were all reluctant to lead. God promises in Hebrews 13:5, ..."Never will I leave you; never will I forsake you." You will be blessed as you serve.

PRAY FOR YOUR GROUP MEMBERS BY NAME.

Before you begin your session, go around the room in your mind, and pray for each member by name. You may want to review the prayer list at least once a week. Ask God to use your time together to touch the heart of every person uniquely. Expect God to lead you to whomever He wants you to encourage or challenge in a special way. If you listen, God will surely lead!

PREPARE FOR YOUR MEETING AHEAD OF TIME.

Review the sessions, Coaching Moments videos, and small group notes. Write down your responses to each question. Finally, review the "Outline for Each Session," so you will remember the purpose of each section in the study.

DO NOT TRY TO DO IT ALONE.

Pray right now for God to help you build a healthy team. If you can enlist a co-leader to help you lead the group, you will find your experience to be much richer. This is your chance to involve as many people as you can in building a healthy group. All you have to do is call and ask people to help. You will probably be surprised at the response.

PROVIDE TRANSITIONS BETWEEN QUESTIONS.

When guiding the discussion, always read aloud the transitional paragraphs and the questions. Ask the group if anyone would like to read the paragraph or Bible passages. Do not call on anyone, but ask for a volunteer and then be patient until someone begins. Be sure to thank the person who reads aloud.

WHEN YOU ASK A QUESTION, BE PATIENT.

Someone will eventually respond. Sometimes people need a moment or two of silence to think about the question. Keep in mind: if silence does not bother you, it will not bother anyone else. After someone responds, affirm the response with a simple "thanks" or "good job." Then ask, "How about somebody else?" Or "Would someone who has not shared like to add anything?" Be sensitive to new people or reluctant members who are not ready to say, pray, or do anything. If you give them a safe setting, they will blossom over time.

ALLOW YOUR EMERGING LEADER(S) TO FACILITATE.

Ask your emerging leaders to facilitate one or more sessions. Give plenty of encouragement and advance notice. You may be perfectly capable of leading each time, but you will help others grow in their faith and gifts if you give them opportunities to lead.

JUST BE YOU.

If you will not be you, who will? God wants you to use your unique gifts and temperament. Do not try to do things exactly like another leader. Do them in a way that fits you! Just admit it when you do not have an answer. Apologize when you make a mistake. Your group will love you for it, and you will sleep better at night!

BREAK UP INTO SMALLER GROUPS TO FACILITATE CONNECTION.

If your group is too large for connection, you may want to have the group gather occasionally in discussion smaller circles during the study. With a greater opportunity to talk in a small circle, people will connect deeper with the study and apply quicker what they are learning. A small circle also encourages a quiet person to participate, and tends to minimize the effects of a more vocal or dominant member. It can also help people feel more loved in your group. When you gather again at the end of the section, you can have one person summarize the highlights from each circle. Small circles are also helpful during prayer time. People who are unaccustomed to praying aloud will feel more comfortable trying it with just two or three others. Also, prayer requests will not take as much time to actually pray. When you gather back with the whole group, you can have one person from each circle briefly update everyone on the prayer requests. People are more willing to pray in small circles if they know the whole group will hear all the prayer requests.

SMALL GROUP ROSTER

SMALL GROUP ROSTER

Name _____

Phone _____

Email _____

Address_____

Notes_____

Name _____

Phone _____

Email _____

Address_____

Notes_____

Name _____

Phone _____

Email _____

Address_____

Notes_____

Name _____

Phone _____

Email _____

Address_____

Notes_____

Name _____

Phone _____

Email _____

Address_____

Notes_____

Name _____

Phone _____

Email _____

Address_____

Notes_____

Name _____

Phone _____

Email _____

Address_____

Notes_____

Name _____

Phone _____

Email _____

Address_____

Notes_____

Name _____

Phone _____

Email _____

Address _____

Notes _____

Name _____

Phone _____

Email _____

Address _____

Notes _____

Name _____

Phone _____

Email _____

Address _____

Notes _____

Name _____

Phone _____

Email _____

Address _____

Notes _____

Name _____

Phone _____

Email _____

Address _____

Notes _____

Name _____

Phone _____

Email _____

Address _____

Notes _____

Name _____

Phone _____

Email _____

Address _____

Notes _____

Name _____

Phone _____

Email _____

Address _____

Notes _____

Name _____

Phone _____

Email _____

Address_____

Notes_____

Name _____

Phone _____

Email _____

Address_____

Notes_____

Name _____

Phone _____

Email _____

Address_____

Notes_____

Name _____

Phone _____

Email _____

Address_____

Notes_____

Name _____

Phone _____

Email _____

Address_____

Notes_____

Name _____

Phone _____

Email _____

Address_____

Notes_____

Name _____

Phone _____

Email _____

Address_____

Notes_____

Name _____

Phone _____

Email _____

Address_____

Notes_____